BEHIND THE WALL STREET CURTAIN

BEHIND THE WALL STREET CURTAIN

Edward Dies

Essay Index Reprint Series

BOOKS FOR LIBRARIES PRESS
FREEPORT, NEW YORK

Reprinted 1969 by arrangement with the
Public Affairs Press and Edward Jerome Dies

ABOUT THE AUTHOR

Business executive, author, and long-time student of finance and investment, Edward Dies formerly held a seat on the Chicago Board of Trade and spent twenty years in Chicago's financial district. He is affiliated with various trade and economic organizations, is a Fellow of the Royal Economic Society, London, a member of the national panel of arbitrators of the American Arbitration Association, and serves with the finance division of the American Society of International Law. He is regarded as an authority on commodity futures markets, and is a strong defender of both stock and commodity exchanges as operated under present laws. He looks upon Wall Street as a symbol of free enterprise, which in turn is a symbol of democracy. He has written this book to dispel popular misconceptions about Wall Street. In his opinion the curtain veiling our financial system is more imagined than real; he is of the conviction it has been devised by superficial economists and vote-seeking politicians.

STANDARD BOOK NUMBER:
8369-1178-4

LIBRARY OF CONGRESS CATALOG CARD NUMBER:
73-86745

PRINTED IN THE UNITED STATES OF AMERICA

CONTENTS

1: Fabulous Lane

Once it was a muddy byway, low-roofed, squalid and repellent. It stretched a quarter of a mile, from old Trinity Church, brooding over its gravestones, to the grimy West India docks on the East River.

Along one side of the narrow, crooked passage was a log wall. So they called it Wall Street, and it became an incredible money lane, the great throbbing heart of finance and commerce, a powerhouse for new industries that helped to build a nation.

Back in the late 1600's it was a highway of swashbuckling pirates, with gay headcloths and huge rings in their ears, and ominous weapons that clanked as they walked. They would nose their craft into the Wall Street Slip and unload sea chests bulging with jewels and other treasures seized in bloody ambushes against rich merchantmen, treasures that helped to enrich early New York.

Arrogant, fearless, and proud of their calling, they would return from a mission and, with pomp and bluster, ride in style to the homes of their clients.

Haughty, and greedy for wealth was the notorious Captain William Kidd, who married a rich widow and became one of the first landed proprietors of the lane and had his home at what is now 56 Wall Street. He was a star among slave traders, and Wall Street was the seat of the slave market. The Captain was a busy broker as blacks from the African Gold Coast were stood up on the auction block at Wall and Water. He would argue convincingly with great merchants in fashionable seventeenth century perukes. He would point out choice human merchandise to proud Lords of the Manor whose crested coaches had whirled them in from sprawling estates.

It was later that Captain Kidd turned pirate, gathered recruits on Wall Street, and began the historic raids in the Indian Ocean, raids that became classic pirate lore. He lived joyously until he exposed his noble patrons and was handed over to the hangman in London.

1

For two and a half centuries people have sung his praise and argued his innocence, and treasure hunters have searched in vain, from the West Indies to Nova Scotia, for his buried wealth of jewels and doubloons.

Time washed the muck and debris from the little street. Eminent families of pre-Revolutionary days built charming homes, even a few mansions, and City Hall, standing directly opposite the cage, pillory and whipping post, added a tone of prestige.

Social change was best recorded by the Merchants Coffee-house on Wall and Water. First it was a rendezvous of slave traders, then of politicians, and then the meeting place of respected merchants who, incidentally, induced the Common Council to wipe out the Slave Market, not for humanitarian reasons, but because it "greatly obstructed the agreeable prospects of the East River which those who live in Wall Street would otherwise enjoy."

As the years ticked off, more and more pious Wall Streeters were going to church. The First Presbyterian — replaced long afterward by the First National Bank — had just concluded services on that April morning in 1775 when a rider from Boston blurted out news of the Battle of Lexington. A hundred of the faithful knelt in the street in prayer.

Their prayers for strength seemed answered in subsequent months as Liberty Boys surged through the street and, on July 18, 1776, jam-packed the narrow byway for the reading of the Declaration of Independence from the steps of City Hall at Wall and Nassau, where the Sub-Treasury now stands.

But hope alone could not stay the force of the enemy and Wall Street was occupied by the British. When they finally turned it back in 1783 it was a heap of rubble and prowling hogs. John Simmons' Tavern was one of the few buildings still standing and here a meeting was held and James Duane was elected the first American mayor of New York.

Hammers rang from dawn to dusk; Trinity was rebuilt on its ruins; new and sturdy office structures arose, to be followed in turn by far more sturdy structures after the great fire of 1835 which laid waste to the highway.

A big lift was given to Wall Street by the decision of the Continental Congress to hold its sessions in City Hall, later rebuilt as Federal Hall, and the great and near-great in law, politics and commerce began settling in the beehive. The immortal Alexander Hamilton, sometimes called the father of the modern Wall Street, opened his law office at what is now 33 Wall, and his uncompromising rival, Aaron Burr, opened up nearby at 10 Cedar Street.

It was to Wall Street that George Washington came in his ruffles and laces and powdered queue in April of 1789 to take the oath of office as first President of the new nation: ". . . I was summoned by my country, whose voice I can never hear but with veneration and love . . ."

He swore to defend the Republic, as he stood proudly on a balcony directly opposite the present Stock Exchange: ". . . that the foundations of our national policy will be laid in the pure and immutable principles of private morality . . ."

For a golden eighteen months the lane of the pirates, the slave traders and the pillory ruled as the capital of the Republic. In that crowded hour of glory Wall Street basked in the light of such brilliant Americans as Jefferson, John Adams, Monroe, Madison, John Hancock, Hamilton and Burr.

And in that crowded hour, too, men turned to Alexander Hamilton for leadership, and his dominating figure moves with sureness and confidence through the commercial records of the time. He established the new nation's credit, set up the first government bank, and sparked one new venture after another that helped drive the infant Republic forward and break the shackles of old world political and commercial domination.

In the yellow fever panic of 1798 Hamilton and Aaron Burr, who rarely agreed on anything, combined in a plan to get permission to create a wholesome water system. The charter, granted to Burr for the purpose, was later found to have a "joker" which permitted Burr's new Manhattan Company to also engage in banking. Thus he cleverly destroyed the Hamilton curtain of banking exclusion, and Burr's Bank of Manhattan Company at 40 Wall Street is today one of the largest privately owned banks; its century and a half of history is studded with the romance of political and economic rivalry.

Yankee genius and industry was on the march. The Merchants' Bank was set up at 25 Wall, the United States at 38 Wall, and other banks followed and fixed the pattern of the future, a pattern that stands as indisputable proof that despite all obstacles, all sins of commission or omission, the course of human events in America is a dynamic course, a course of progress.

Strong men captained the ships of business and finance, men whose deeds were too often lost in the shadows while spotlights played on speculative frenzies of the hour. For every sound venture there were men of courage to drive it to success; for every invention there stood a man of industry ready to snatch it from the bench and put it into production.

Little wheels of industry began to whirr in the third year of Washington's first administration, at a time when New York's forty thousand inhabitants occupied five square miles.

Laws of finance by the first Congress had brought the need of a market place for securities. So in 1792 twenty-four, brokers had formed a stock exchange and selected a daily meeting place. It was under the broad branches of an old buttonwood tree at what is now 68 Wall Street. In the shade of that tree they dealt in government "stock," and in a few issues of bank, insurance and canal shares.

It was a quarter of a century later, a day of great pride and rejoicing, that the brokers adopted a constitution and took the New York Stock Exchange indoors, into modest quarters at the old Tontine Coffee-house. Eleven other moves were made and then the Exchange settled in its present quarters.

Years passed before there were any dramatic profits for brokers. Dull days registered trading as low as thirty-one shares. But with the coming of industrial shares, and later the railroads, volume became substantial and Exchange membership expanded to meet public needs. As late as 1878 a membership could be purchased for $4,000, as against $625,000 in 1929, and $17,000 in the market dogdays of 1942. Not in fifty years has the percentage solvency of Stock Exchange members slipped below 99. In depression's depth of 1932 it was 99.78, against 92.36 for all U. S. banks.

In the Wall Street story may be found the record of the astonishing industrial rise of a new nation. From the first stirrings of the industrial age Wall Street was the lender directly or indirectly to the cattle man, the ship builder, the cotton spinner, the sheep herder and the builder of railroads.

Lenders are usually despised in periods of credit collapse and denounced by rabble rousers and chest-beating politicians. It is nothing new. It reaches back to far off Mesopotamia where peddlers who swapped jade for skins, and sometimes made advance loans, were hated by plainsmen when markets turned sour. In the early records the back of the lender was no stranger to the lash, and gibbets were set up in market places as grim reminders to the sinful.

But Wall Sstreet remained the lender, the throbbing pulse of the world's greatest industrial miracle. The Stock Exchange provided the auction place for securities and helped pump venture capital into new mills and plants and factories. Today the wires of its 1,375 members pattern the nation, and its listed securities, including bonds, have a value of over two hundred billion dollars. Half the people of the land have an interest in those securities, either as shareholders or holders of insurance policies or bank accounts.

Faint rumblings of the onrushing industrial expansion at the turn of the nineteenth century alerted a race of men with courage and vision. They were the product of a new civilization that put a premium on freedom and liberty and individual initiative. They harnessed steam to machines, lifted clumsy tools from the hands of craftsmen, and started wheels spinning in plants and mills. In the first quarter of that century they brought an avalanche of power appliances to basic industries.

Genius of the Yankee brand — scientific, mechanical, commercial and financial — swept forward, and for fifty years under the leadership of the Lawrences, Abbotts, Brookses, Browns, Astors and Vanderbilts American initiative and enterprise astonished the world and lighted hope in the hearts of men.

Like a flood, the huge industrial economy began spreading across the land and Wall Street and the Stock Exchange mirrored the day to day progress. Vital, alive, they poured forth the venture capital, distributed the risks, and evaluated the consequences.

Out of the Street came funds to build the railroads, to develop the West, to revivify faltering trades; funds to create new industries with the discovery of petroleum, copper, silver and other metals; funds to build still other industries — telephone, gas, electric — and a veritable river of capital to meet the needs of yet another miracle known as mass production.

Far beyond the puny efforts of individual man, the collateral drive of a nation, under the untrammeled principle of free enterprise, lifted a people to the highest standard of living ever known to the world. Out of the little street of the slave market, the byway of the pirates, came an unparalleled system of banking and exchange.

Yet every forward impulse of magnitude had its seamy side. That was a part of the price of progress. With a cold daring akin to that of the early pirates, the notorious manipulators — the Drews, the Fisks, the Goulds and the Littles — stormed across the high seas of finance and dragooned the markets with a reckless fury. Their glaring misdeeds remained a blotch on the Wall Street record for nearly a century.

Still the early sins of Wall Street were school boy capers compared to the dreadful promotions of "bubble" companies of an earlier day in England and France. At one time a hundred and four of these spurious companies were listed: companies to make salt water fresh, to build hospitals for bastard children, to trade in human hair, to extract silver from lead, to manufacture perpetual motion, and strangest of all, a company "whose purpose will be revealed later." In the first hour a thousand people poured their money into the latter company, and that evening the projector levanted. On one day in Paris so great was the crowd in the street clamoring to get into John Law's office with their money that a little hunchback earned 50,000 francs by allowing eager speculators to use his hump as a desk. Said Voltaire:

"I have seen John Law come to court, followed humbly by dukes, by marshals and by bishops."

Stockjobbers and their wives drove gorgeous coaches, decked with brand new coats of arms; they and their wives were suddenly admitted to exclusive circles, and aped the manners and vices of the aristocracy who courted them for favor; that is, until the bubbles burst and the black days came on.

Wall Street's Arabian Nights ended long ago, tapered off, to be followed by the creation of huge trusts, which in turn were broken up by court orders and by inflexible laws to banish monopoly. The curtain finally dropped on unsavory manipulations and thereafter, for a long period, Wall Street earned and held a large measure of public respect.

From Harvard, Yale and Princeton young men of family came down to the Street for prosaic careers in banking and securities. The great brokerage houses were dignified, aloof, and made no particular drive for business. A few stretched a point by permitting their names to appear in so-called tombstone ads in the financial pages of the papers.

But all this dignity and public prestige was suddenly swept away in the 1929 debacle, probably the last big speculative outcropping in American stock market history. For the politicians took over with a vengeance, as they always do when they sense public sentiment. They enacted many laws on banking and stock trading, some of them excellent and in the public interest.

But politicians rarely know when to stop, and the loud outcries after the collapse were grist to their mills. They demanded more and more government intervention into finance, commerce and industry. They enacted laws that put the government deeper and deeper into numerous enterprises requiring more and more money. As early as 1949 tax collections for the country as a whole averaged $1,073 for each family. For the previous peace-time calendar year the staggering collections of the Federal internal revenue were equal to all the wages and salaries of some fifteen million workers employed in all the mines and factories of the country.

Leaders of finance stood aghast as venture capital for new industries continued to shrink, to be sucked up in higher taxes. Wall Street wondered whether it was paying anew for its sins of long ago, or whether a definite plan existed for adopting some old world pattern of statism. Chief hope lay in the magnificent greed of the American people for freedom and liberty and individual initiative.

Meantime, the narrow canyon of Wall Street is still busy by day and empty and eerie with loneliness at night. And old Trinity, silent among its tombstones, awaits the next chapter in the colorful story of the fabulous lane.

2: First Big Raid

Thomas Jefferson, author of the Declaration of Independence, was thundering his anger at the great Alexander Hamilton:

"It's monstrous," he stormed, "that this country should be ruled by a foreign bastard."

Like others, Jefferson was decrying the base and ignoble speculative raid — first in the nation's history — which was incident to Hamilton's funding of the national debt.

Amid cyclones of abuse and charges of fraud, Hamilton, first Secretary of the Treasury, had gone stolidly forward and had set up the most magnificent financial structure ever conceived by man. He had lifted a new and wavering nation out of bankruptcy and firmly established the public credit.

Jefferson, a son of aristocracy, believed in domination of the masses. Hamilton, a son of the masses, believed in the rule of aristocracy. There was no bridge to span the gap of their conflicting philosophies; yet each made monumental contributions to democracy.

Of Hamilton's "marvelous precocity" John Fiske, the historian, wrote: "His intellect seemed to have sprung forth in full maturity."

But even in his splendid hour of lofty achievement, Hamilton was not permitted by critics to forget that he was born out of wedlock, in a British colony of the West Indies.

His mother, Rachel Fawcett, with sparkling gray eyes and fair hair tinged with red, was the daughter of a wealthy physician and planter, and was educated in languages, music and art. Her parents had separated, and at sixteen she had been coerced by her mother into marriage with an older man, a Dane of wealth and social position. She had been presented at court and received in Copenhagen society, but after a short period, in a fit of revulsion, she had fled back to the West Indies. A few years later, at Nevis, she met James Hamilton, an educated, well-born Scottish gentleman. They fell

8

deeply in love, and after repeated futile efforts to free Rachel from
her unfortunate marriage they decided, with the blessing of Nevis
society, to unite outside the law.

Of this union Alexander Hamilton, one of the world's great
statesmen, was born on January 11, 1757; and when his young mother
died eleven years later he was sent to live with Ann Mitchell, an
aunt, while his unsuccessful father sought new business ventures on
neighboring islands.

With no apparent effort, the slim, dark boy absorbed knowledge
with amazing rapidity — languages, mathematics, literature, philosophy. At twelve he was engaged by Nicholas Cruger, largest merchant in the Caribbees, whose ships, laden with timber, sugar and
rum plied the distant seas. At fourteen he was left in full charge of
the business during long absences of Cruger. The boy determined
cargoes of imports and exports, decided when to buy and sell for
foreign clients, and ordered the arming of ships against possible
attacks.

Then a strange thing happened. A terrible hurricane swept St.
Croix, and young Hamilton's colorful story of the storm immediately
riveted attention upon his brilliant intellect. With the aid of the
resident governor, relatives got together some funds and sent him off
to the states to study. He never returned.

His every act glinted of genius — his studies at King's College
(now Columbia University), his impassioned pre-war speeches, his
work as aide to Washington in the Revolutionary War, to which post
he was appointed at twenty, his study of law, and his service in
Congress.

When Washington became President he induced Hamilton, then
thirty-two, to give up a lucrative law practice and serve as Secretary
of the Treasury at less than one-third his current income. By that
time Hamilton ranked with Washington, Jefferson and Franklin as
one of the four great Americans of his day.

Money matters were in a mess. The Confederacy had gone
down the financial toboggan and, in the words of one historian, the
Union was "bankrupt and hastening to dissolution." The public debt
was mountainous for those days. Paper had been issued by the Continental Congress with utter disregard for repayment, and the values
of various other outstanding certificates were tumbling rapidly. In
all the world's history, say some scholars, no statesman ever had to
cope with so great a task with such small resources.

Hamilton knew what the country needed. He had proclaimed

his views long before in articles in The Federalist. He would fight for redemption of every borrowed dollar, for assumption of state debts, for a single stable currency, for a central banking system, and for government support of commerce and industry.

"States, like individuals, who observe their engagements are respected and trusted," he wrote. "The reverse is true of those who pursue an opposite conduct." Political independence, he insisted, was but a myth without national financial security.

His report to Congress, which he was instructed to prepare three weeks after taking office, has been long regarded as a masterpiece, a foundation stone for a system that has stood the test of volcanic economic changes.

Weeks before Hamilton's report was submitted to the House and Senate in January, 1790, speculators were laying the groundwork for a gigantic raid. The opportunity for plunder and profit was obvious. Thousands of persons, scattered over wide areas, held an immense volume of paper, both in the form of currency and script. Soldiers of the Revolution had been given script for back-pay as well as for liberal bonuses. They had returned to their mills and their farms with a sense of security. But after a few years they had found it impossible to pass along this government paper, and as the phrase "not worth a continental" gained in popularity, they resigned themselves to the loss.

Speculators filled the galleries and the lobbies when the Hamilton report was read to the members of Congress. Some members received it with deep concern. Senator William Maclay of Pennsylvania wrote that he himself "was struck of a heap." Another Senator complained that a committee of speculators "could not have formed the report more to their advantage."

Wild rejoicing did indeed sweep through the speculative ranks. In anticipation of such a report separate syndicates had been formed in New York, Boston and Philadelphia and their agents had raced through the country buying up government paper at from ten to twenty cents on the dollar. A golden field was found in the outlying districts and the interior, which were always weeks behind on current happenings. Farmers, soldiers and merchants, the original holders of the paper, embraced the occasion to unload on the busy speculators.

Hamilton's report had been divided into two parts. The first part called for the funding of all government securities at par. The second part provided for assumption by the government of State debts.

Irate legislators roared their wrath at the first part of the report, which would refund the government certificates at par with interest-bearing bonds. They rightly pointed out that this would give the speculators rich and wicked profits on their raids. At the same time it would necessitate new taxation to pay the interest, and such taxes would fall heavily upon the same soldiers, small merchants and farmers who had been bilked.

Patriotic editors, while recognizing the critical need for a sound financial system, likewise cried out against the speculative raid. The *New York Daily Advertiser* declared that if the funding plan carried banker Robert Morris stood to win $18,000,000, Jeremiah Wadsworth $9,000,000 and Governor George Clinton of New York $5,000,000. John Quincy Adams wrote to his father that Christopher Gore, a Hamilton party aide in Massachusetts, had already "made an independent fortune in speculation. . . ."

In the long and stormy fight on the floor Hamilton brooked no compromise. His leaders howled down objections. Some of them did so with selfish reason, for it was brought out long afterward that twenty-nine of the sixty-four House members were security holders. Such speculative indulgence was distasteful to Hamilton. He admitted that poor men who had parted with their paper from necessity were to be pitied. But he felt no sympathy for those who had let go their securities from lack of faith in government redemption, and he stated quite boldly that the purchaser "ought to reap the benefit of his hazard" for he did, after all, carry the risk.

With indominable will the audacious Hamilton drove the refunding bill to enactment. And speculators in the Wall Street coffeehouses tossed their hats in the air and danced with joy.

America's first big speculative raid had been a glowing success.

For the next part of Hamilton's program the going was much more rugged. Southern states with strong financial positions were bitterly opposed to the leveling down process incident to government assumption of state debts. They meant to beat the plan.

Speculators felt otherwise. They had faith in the growing power of Hamilton. Syndicates of wealthy men, working with members of Congress, sent more express riders galloping into the wilderness to buy up the "worthless" paper. When millions of dollars worth of the state securities had been gathered in the cities the speculators sat back and waited for the rise.

But an unexpected thunderbolt incident to a vote on the "assumption" bill struck the money pools. The bill was beaten and the great Hamilton went down to his first defeat. Speculators at first were panic-stricken and visualized the wiping out of all their previous gains. They held firm their lines, however. Their one hope rested upon Hamilton's ability to realign his forces and bring the measure to a second test.

Tireless, determined and with no show of discouragement Hamilton labored for the next three months against heavy odds, and with no success in the way of changing the necessary handful of opposition votes. Then in June of 1790 the Secretary of State, Thomas Jefferson, returned from France. Hamilton knew that Jefferson nursed an overpowering desire to have the national capitol moved to Georgetown after a ten-year period in Philadelphia. He wanted the capitol for the south as deeply and sincerely as Hamilton wanted his financial program adopted. The terms, then, were simple; the two men met and talked, and a deal was consummated. Hamilton was given the six votes needed — one in the Senate and five in the House. In return he pledged his support to Jefferson's plan for the capitol. The assumption bill was enacted into law on August 4, 1790, and the syndicates made their second spectacular killing, piling up new millions in profits.

It was long afterward that Jefferson, who had broken with Hamilton, made his withering personal attacks upon the Secretary of the Treasury. Historians say these belated attacks came with poor grace in the light of Jefferson's part in the program. Said Jefferson:

"When the trial of strength had indicated the form in which the bill would finally pass, this being known within doors sooner than without, especially than to those who were in distant parts of the Union, the base scramble began. Couriers and relay horses by land, and swift-sailing boats by sea, were flying in all directions. Active partners and agents were associated and employed in every state, town and country neighborhood; and this paper was bought for five shillings and even as low as two shillings, in the pound, before the holder knew that Congress had already provided for its redemption at par. Immense sums were thus filched from the poor and ignorant, and fortunes accumulated by those who had themselves been poor enough before."

It was indeed the wily Jeremiah Wadsworth, member of Congress from Connecticut, a banking associate of Hamilton, who had freighted two fast sloops with coin and sent them racing for paper at distant points in the south.

But Hamilton's honesty never was successfully challenged. Remorseless, indiscreet and autocratic, he held to his single purpose —

adoption of the program. If his brother-in-law, John B. Church, and his wife's father, General Philip Schuyler, profitted along with other leaders of the Revolutionary period, that was not his affair. Everyone knew that he entered office a poor man, left office a poorer man, and was still poor when he died on the dueling field at the age of forty-seven years.

The cold, indisputable facts lay in his record. In less than six years in office he had created for the country a complete fiscal administration, a solid, massive financial structure that stood the strain of unprecedented growth. His program stands today a masterpiece of singular genius.

Hamilton, the statesman and business man, was no politician. He was a driver rather than a leader of men. He burned with lofty ambition and was short and impatient with those who opposed him. He made bitter enemies, among them Aaron Burr, another aggressive man of fiery sureness and proud and passionate temperament.

They were born ten months apart, were the same height within an inch, and their weight varied by but five pounds. Each had a brilliant military record. In the drawing room their wit, courtly manners, and low, alluring voices turned the heads of women. On the platform, in public debate, or at the bar of justice the magic of their words held listeners spellbound. It was inevitable that jealousy and smouldering hatred should sometime burst into flame.

Hamilton struck the first painful blow. When Burr ran for the Presidency in 1800 he received the same number of electoral votes as Jefferson. This left the selection up to Congress. Hamilton, with no other choice, threw his weight to the side of Jefferson and the latter won. Burr was named Vice President.

Hamilton still smarted under the sting of new innuendoes by Burr and his lieutenants with respect to Hamilton's part in the speculative raids. And he continued to strike back at Burr as each opportunity arose. When Vice President Burr sought to become governor of New York as a sure road to the next Presidential nomination, Hamilton openly and bitterly opposed him. As a consequence once again Burr suffered a soul-shaking defeat. His wrath knew no bounds. He sent a note asking an explanation of certain language used against him and on receipt of an evasive reply from Hamilton he issued a challenge. Hamilton chose pistols at ten paces.

For the historic duel they met at seven o'clock on the morning of July 10, 1804, on the heights of Weehauken, overlooking New York Bay. On the identical spot three years earlier Hamilton's son Philip, eldest of eight children and with much of his father's fire and talent, had fallen in a duel as a result of having heckled a Burr speaker. The shock had deranged the mind of his sister Angelica.

Both Burr and Hamilton were pale, but free of visible nervousness. Hamilton won the toss for choice of positions. Pacing off the thirty feet with cocked pistols, the men then turned and faced each other. At the signal Burr's shot rang out, followed by Hamilton's overhead shot. Instantly Hamilton rose convulsively on his toes, reeled and collapsed. He died the following day.

Said the *Charleston* (S.C.) *Courier*: "Even Washington's passing was not so great a loss to the nation."

Said another Southern editor: "A colossus of might he stood, the American commonwealth on his shoulders."

3: Daniel Drew : The Spoiler

There he stands, a lean, hymn singing, tobacco chewing old hypo-crite, cackling merrily at his own jokes. There he stands in history, Daniel Drew, the drover, the circus clown, the notorious Wall Street buccaneer, whose staggering speculations emptied treasuries and rocked the world of finance.

Down the years, for nearly a century, his sinister shadow has clouded Wall Street, for he was a destroyer, a symbol of all that is bad in speculation, an uncommon American with an uncommon genius for fiscal trickery. Of him it was said: "There is less of every-thing when he passes by."

His speculative toys were steamboat lines and railroads and gold and the bonds of his government. He was a Bear, a pessimist who fattened on national turmoil and distress. He amassed millions in forty years of market rigging, built churches to mirror his purity of heart, and died broke at 82 whining sanctimoniously that "too few men attend prayer meetin'."

This tall, physically tough farmer boy, born of good parents in 1797 alongside Whangton Brook near Carmel, New York, was a master of guile and cunning even in childhood. His first recorded deal was in 1814 when at seventeen he sold himself as a draft substitute for a hundred dollars, served a few months, and then demanded the money back from his widowed mother to enter the illegal "bob veal" business, in which ugly traffic he prospered.

It consisted of buying up newly-dropped calves and rushing them to market on wobbly legs before they stopped breathing. The flesh was so soft that buyers used to complain it "could be sucked through a quill." Farmers complained, too, that Danny faded from scene to scene without always lifting the tab of indebtedness; and so after a few years he joined the circus.

Preachers at that time were thundering against these sinful new

15

Rolling Shows, but, even so, the church trade grew in volume as Drew bellowed the glories, not of the circus, but of his "Great Moral Exhibition." They roared at the antics of Drew the Clown. Butchers gave him free meat for the lions in return for mere mention of their names from the ring. Men of the Cloth who had linked circuses with Hell Fire were somewhat deflated one night when the Clown himself marched boldly down the church aisle and loudly gave his soul to God.

Flushed with the Spirit, his pockets well lined, Brother Drew at length resumed the drover business with vigor, and was astonished and delighted at the profitable farmer reaction to his glib quotations from the Bible.

"Good morning, Brother Jones. The peace of God be on you. How you fixed for fat stock?"

They even gave him credit. And money rolled in. He moved rapidly from district to district. It averted many hot squabbles over past deals.

His busy mind fashioned quaint tricks for selling herds to the New York City butchers. He would drive a herd for two days without water, then feed salt all night, and next morning let the parched beasts drink their fill just before buyers appeared. On one such costly deal, the only reason butcher Henry Astor, brother of John Jacob Astor, did not dispatch the wily Drew was inability to find him. "He's like a flea." Wall Street took the phrase "watered stock" from this drover's trick.

Drew was in his mid-thirties before steamboats struck his fancy. He had married Roxana Mead in 1820, and later taken her to Bull's Head Tavern which he operated on the Boston Post Road, a hangout for drovers, who liked the lively tap room, the games of chance, and the turkey shoots in which they were invited to engage, especially if their vision had first been conditioned in the tap room. Mine host was also village banker, and he made occasional long trips into the midwest for herds that swelled his exchequer for the big steamboat wars ahead.

Early steamboating was a bitter, cut-throat business. There was gun play between rival pilots; races that burst engines; rate wars that sometimes granted free passage — a setting styled to the talents of Daniel Drew.

And the field was wide open after the Supreme Court, in the famous Gibbons vs. Ogden suit of 1824, had smashed the vicious Fulton-Livingston monopoly, a monopoly backed by a brazen Legislature that had barred outside vessels from plying State waters "by fire or steam."

It was five years later that young Captain Cornelius Vanderbilt started his own Hudson River boat. As Drew lolled on the deck chatting gaily during trips up to his Drewclift farm at Carmel, he coveted his friend's prosperity. So he took corrective measures: He invested in a rival company and with his steamer *Water Witch* tried to run Vanderbilt's *Cinderella* off the river. But he lost ten thousand dollars; then he raised money from farmers to "fight the monopoly for the public" and, still unsuccessful, quietly sold out to Vanderbilt and let angry stockholders shout themselves tired. "An egg today means a hen tomorrow."

Vanderbilt broke with the Hudson River Association, placed rival boats on the Albany run and made things so hot they bought him out. Drew quickly took this cue. He put two rival boats on the run and forced the Association to make him a director. But why stop here? Under a dummy he launched a new cut-rate boat that hurt his own company so much the directors urged him to make a deal with the mysterious rival.

"I'll see the rascal at once," he said, seizing his hat. "He's only a spit and a stride from here."

Around the corner Drew consulted himself for a few minutes. Then he burst in upon the directors with glad tidings. He had closed the deal, he said, for eight thousand more (which he pocketed). Later he split with the group, purchased ships that out-raced their prize craft, and finally bought up the company. With Isaac Newton he founded the People's Line, and for forty years his name was linked with proud ships that glided up and down the water lane playing gay tunes and sometimes missing advertised stops in their zeal for speed records.

Thus a Wall Street magnate was born.

Prayer meeting hymns beat in his veins like gypsy music as Drew moved onward and upward. His brokerage firm of Drew, Robinson and Company prospered, for Robinson, an ex-circus hand, also was nimble with ship and rail shares. Drew by this time was perfectly adjusted in his new brownstone house on Union Square, with a shed behind for a cow and for his shiny black horse which he drove clip-clop to Wall Street in a doctor's buggy. Let the money crowd snarl at his ethics. Wasn't he a Brother in the church, and hadn't he just put up money for a new edifice?

"I was busy as a dog lickin' a dish, and I never cared what people said. . . . My one dream then was to control Erie Railroad."

This goal he attained with rare cunning. First he gave preferred steamer rates to the competing New York Central lines. Next he seized control of Lake Erie steamers upon whose western service Erie had depended; and finally he bought the Buffalo and State Line Railroad and thus completely boxed in the Erie at both ends.

"Mr. Drew," said the Committee, "we would be honored to have you serve on our directorate."

Happy day. At last he was an insider and ready to start his shocking deals that made Erie known as "The Scarlet Woman of Wall Street."

Money poured in from his endless raids, manipulations that sometimes found the mighty Vanderbilt, the Bull, the builder, the roaring extrovert, on the opposite side of the market; for three decades the two giants battled over the spoils of speculation.

But to be a mere director was not enough. Drew wanted Erie in his pants pocket. So again he read the stars and set his course. The directors had determined to take the line into Jersey City and tunnel through Bergen Hill. Pretending agreement, the crafty Drew secretly obstructed the project, almost, but not quite, to the point of preventing it. Alarming rumors came from Albany that a charter would be refused; Wall Street was flooded with reports that the tunnel was a death trap; prices of Erie shares began to tumble, dividends were reduced, and the road was forced to borrow funds quickly.

So Drew himself humbly offered the loan (for a mortgage on the rolling stock, of course). "Mr. Drew," said the sad Committee, "we would be honored to have you serve as Treasurer of the road." That night at prayer meeting, back in 1851, Brother Drew sang:

> Glory to God who treads the sky,
> And sends his blessings through;
> Who tells his saints of joys on high,
> And gives a taste below.

Vanderbilt looked upon railroads as a practical way of getting across the country. Drew saw them only as a speculative toy. When he seized control, Erie was a thriving property, America's pride, longest and best railroad in the world, with many English stockholders. Before he had finished, the road had been squeezed dry of funds, its

rolling stock run down, its road bed flimsy and highly dangerous.
"I'm happiest," he chuckled, "when the market's singin' a lullaby."

Treasurer Drew had all the inside secret information as well as
the road's funds with which to speculate. By a mere whisper he could
send stock prices up or down to his liking. In the words of the Street,
he could even make Erie shares wiggle-waggle. While his personal
wealth piled high he found no funds available for replacing thin rails.
And rails were snapping and wrecking trains and people were dying
in burning coaches that tumbled over embankments.

"There's too much sin today, card playin' and theater goin',"
wailed the almost illiterate Mr. Drew. He was just starting another
church and underwriting the Drew Theological Seminary, at the opening of which he basked in the warm light of extravagant praise:
". . . that the good Lord might give us more Daniel Drews."

Of the endless deals, many of which were joined by his able
pupils, Jim Fisk and Jay Gould, one in 1866 best typifies his methods.
Erie needed three and a half million dollars. As security they en-
trusted to Treasurer Drew a block of unissued stock and three million
dollars of convertible bonds. Drew began selling Erie stock short at
95 and continued as the market zoomed upward in a wave of buying.
He looked sad and worried (Drew was a good actor) and the Street
danced in glee when he seemed to be cornered and ruined. But at
last he struck with lightning quickness. He appropriated the three
million dollars of bonds, converted them to stock, poured it all on the
market, sent Erie shares crashing to 50, covered his short sales, and
came up with millions of dollars in profits.

Drew learned everything worth knowing about market rigging,
even in Civil War days when, beardless, he looked like a dishonest
Abe Lincoln. With the nation's life hanging by a thread he thundered
through the markets with mighty short sales on the heels of every
Union defeat. Telegraphers were bribed for advance news.

"It's good fishin' in troubled waters," said the cold-blooded old
stock jobber. "War gave me my richest four years."

More and more he became Wall Street's enemy number one.
He fought disastrous battles with Vanderbilt over Harlem railroad
stock; then the two titans locked horns over control of Erie and, in
1867, the battle ended with Drew expelled from the directorate;
domination of Erie passed, strangely enough, to his pupil Jay Gould.

The master was losing his touch. One raid after another — the
"lock up" of greenbacks, an attempted Erie corner in 1868, and other
abortive sallies — cut deeply into his holdings. Finally he had broken

with Gould and was now an outsider, but in one last flair of singular genius caught Gould heavily short and squeezed him unmercifully.

When feelings had cooled off, the velvety Mr. Gould visited Uncle Daniel, talked quietly and soothingly of the good old days, of their happy years together, and then revealed his plan for a "bull" movement in Erie and a "bear" movement in Northwestern and invited his dear old friend to join in the golden harvest.

Perhaps the tired, aging master was growing soft and less alert; or perhaps the many lawsuits and the blustering creditors were distorting his mental processes. In any case he swallowed the bait. And when the trap snapped it was too late.

For what Mr. Gould had actually set up was a "bear" movement in Erie and a "bull" movement in Northwestern, the reverse of what he had told Drew. Both deals came off with clock-like precision. In the case of Northwestern Gould had cornered the market at 105 and then whipped it upward to 230, at which point Brother Drew forked over another million dollars.

Rejoicing swept the Street. Headlines said "the curse" had at long last been removed. It was indeed the beginning of the end, the foggy twilight of a dishonorable career, for along came the 1873 panic and down went a Drew house, Kenyon, Cox and Company, and down went Jay Cooke and Company, and a national crash followed.

The curtain was falling on the drama of Daniel Drew. When an attempted gold corner brought him only public denunciation, and a flyer in Wabash cost him another half million dollars he knew that for him the market had sung a final lullaby. Quickly he mortgaged his house, hid what small assets he could, before he was declared a bankrupt.

Back at Carmel he mooned around the countryside, trying to find peace. In time the magnet of speculation drew him back to the Street, where former friends shunned him and where brokers refused small credits. From the Hoffman House he dabbled in a few stocks, and later had a stock ticker set up in the basement of a house. At prayer meetings he sang his favorite hymn:

> From every stormy wind that blows,
> From every swelling tide of woes,
> There is a calm, a sure retreat,
> 'Tis found beneath the mercy seat.

He died in 1879. To the Street the unbeautiful old clown bequeathed a pattern of stock jobbing never equalled in history.

4: James Fisk, Jr. : Happy Hatchet Man

Beautiful women, voluptuous and desirable, moved in and out of the life of handsome Jim Fisk. Blondes, brunettes, red heads . . . bejeweled and gowned to the pinnacle of silky perfection. Calloused Wall Street sometimes blinked as they gathered for champagne luncheons in Fisk's plushy office while crashing markets spread business ruin.

Gay ladies were a part of the equipment of the swashbuckling speculator, like his glittering carriages and his elegant, if slightly spurious, uniforms.

"Girls never hurt anyone," roared Jubilee Jim. But that was before he met Josie, long before two bullets put a violent and dramatic end to a spectacular career. It was, indeed, about the time that James A. Garfield, heading a Congressional committee, was reporting: "The malign influence which Catiline wielded over the reckless youth of Rome finds a fitting parallel in the power which Fisk held in Wall Street, when, followed by the thugs of Erie and the debauchees of the opera, he swept into the Gold Room and defied both the Street and the Treasury."

But that Gold Conspiracy really belonged to Jay Gould who, like Daniel Drew, used Fisk as hatchet man in certain titanic manipulations. The three men went down as the trickiest triumvirate in speculative history. Fisk left no great fortune, only a million dollars to his widow, but in his brief, diamond studded, spendthrift career he was perhaps as well known as any man in America.

Big blonde James Fisk, Jr., with his wavy hair and needlepoint mustache, was a gaudy, dashing charlatan whose quick tongue tossed off belly-shaking wisecracks. He was irresistible and irrepressible.

His stepmother had seen to it that he picked up a bit of schooling at Brattleboro, Vermont, to which the family had moved from

21

Bennington where he was born in 1834; and for her tender consideration Fisk remembered her in his will.

He held no lofty regard, however, for his father, a country peddler, but did join him for a brief and restless period after a stretch as a circus handyman. He found his father's sales methods so stodgy and boring that he struck out on his own and before long he had four wagons, all painted in brilliant colors and drawn by prancing steeds; just like circus carts. They would converge on a village, with a brass band, and the flashily dressed huckster would load down the yokels with his wares — dress goods, silks, shawls, jewelry and Yankee notions.

Success so impressed his Boston supply house, Jordan and Marsh, that they gave him a job, a job in which he was most unhappy until along came the Civil War. Then he sensed at once that the government needed blankets. And he found that the firm had a huge supply, of fine quality, piled in a storeroom.

Thereupon Jim Fisk met a Boston lady who knew some congressmen. Soon he set off for Washington with letters and a fat purse. He sold the blankets and he sold so many other things that the firm had to expand its mills and plants; and since some of the contracts were drawn in his own name the company found it expedient to make him a partner.

He was a blatant, daring partner, slightly shocking to the sensibilities of a respected house, but a big money maker, nonetheless, for himself and for others, especially with his cotton smuggling from the South. Jordan and Marsh finally were glad to move him out — for a consideration of $60,000.

He opened his own showy store, but post-war inflation hit hard; then he tackled Wall Street and was cleaned in a few weeks. Back in Boston he tried to settle down with a wife, Lucy Moore, a kindly, considerate woman who let him lead his hectic life free of domestic handicaps.

But Wall Street was in his blood and he was soon back there introducing himself as The Prince of Peddlers to Daniel Drew and offering to sell a stack of Stonington Steamboat shares with which Drew had been stuck. Said Drew:

"The young scalawag was brisk as a bottle of ale. His big hands were covered with rings. I saw he was a comer. He quickly unloaded those shares and many others."

So Drew set him up, with William Belden, son of a "camp meeting shouter", as his private broker in Erie railroad shares, and later put him on the board of directors. Before long Jim Fisk was a new meteor lighting the skies of finance.

In one of his many appearances before investigating bodies he testified: "My business is railroading, steamboating, and I suppose I may add, speculating."

He might well have added: political fixer with the crooked Tweed Ring, briber of courts and legislatures, and in the words of Henry Ward Beecher, "supreme mountebank of fortune" — a shrewd, generous, apostle of fraud who could have existed only in the corrupt and convulsive Seventies.

The chronicle of his astonishing raids on Wall Street is tangled and knotted; the affairs of magnitude mostly tie in with Drew and Gould. Some strange bond pulled the three together. Yet each distrusted and, on occasion, skinned the others with brazen unconcern and with his own special kind of fiscal genius.

In the tight spots Fisk had a quick intuitive mind, brilliant and resourceful, that lighted the avenue of escape when all roads were closed. There was, for instance, the unholy manipulation of 1868.

Cornelius Vanderbilt was planning the consolidation of the Hudson River and Central roads. Among other things he wanted the three swindlers chased out of Erie. Specifically he wanted them to issue no more stocks, nor convert more bonds into stocks until after repaying the road large sums already stolen. To this end he secured various injunctions.

"Injunctions be damned!" bellowed Fisk. "Sweet Jesus. We can get injunctions too."

Whereupon the three Erie officials met in secret, as the Executive Committee, issued $10,000,000 in bonds, and converted them into stock on Fisk's private printing press. Fisk then "stole" the certificates from a messenger as a technicality to keep them free of injunctions. Then they were dumped onto a rising market in which Vanderbilt was buying every share offered.

Meantime, in the deep of night, crooked judges were issuing injunctions against the Vanderbilt injunction. Moaned one paper: ". . . the most disgraceful prostitution of legal forms ever witnessed."

Vanderbilt soon found himself loaded with $7,000,000 of spurious Erie stock. Nearly $5,000,000 had been paid in cash. He was in the tightest position of his stormy career.

Next day, with sheriffs close on their heels, Fisk said: "Boys, it's hot. We're moving to Jersey City, bag and baggage. That's foreign ground. They can't touch us there."

In a wild scramble they piled Erie accounts, records, books and stacks of Vanderbilt greenbacks into a hack and, under cover of a deep fog, raced for the ferry. Fisk, a fearless wolf, tarried for dinner with a singer and barely escaped by rowboat in the night.

Settled snug and cozy in the Ladies Parlor of Taylor's Hotel ("I like the location"), Fisk boomed to his frightened companions: "Cheer up, my hearties. Naught is lost save honor. We have the chink, we'll bear the stink."

There was real reason for fear. Messengers rushed in with word that an army of hired thugs would try to cross the river and drag the trio back to Ludlow Street Jail. Jim Fisk flew into action. He barricaded "Fort Taylor" and placed Drew in charge of ground forces. Gould was to handle all railroad matters and keep the trains running. "Admiral" Fisk himself took charge of the navy — four boatloads of men armed with rifles. On a dock two twelve-pounders were mounted. In no time he had the place crawling with police, Erie detectives and paid volunteers.

The enemy viewed the scene and wisely delayed attack.

Amid a new blizzard of court orders, Gould sneaked off to Albany with a satchel of money, and the Senate — termed by the New York Independent "an assemblage of official thieves" — passed a bill legalizing the new Erie stock. But before the lower house had acted, both sides in the battle revolted against the high cost of bribery and got together on these terms:

Contempt of court charges were withdrawn. Vanderbilt was relieved of the bad stock. Fisk and his partners kept their "short sale" profits. Drew agreed to quit as a director, and Erie control passed to Fisk and Gould. In the final pay-off about $9,000,000 was involved. It was drained from Erie's treasury. Fisk did not regard the terms of settlement as entirely honest, as he testified later: "A paper was passed around and I signed it in disgust. . . . I felt I had sold myself to the devil."

But Jim Fisk never feared the devil for long; not even in his wars over the Albany and Susquehanna. In these conflicts violence flared to a point where rival engines were charging each other over a disputed right of way. And in one bit of personal combat Fisk was thrown headlong down a stairway in Albany and later, disguised, narrowly escaped a crowd of angry men close at heel.

To burly, boisterous Jim it was all great fun, and his nerves of steel never jangled, even under pressure of such sensational manipulations as the historic greenback lock-up. For he was a happy man.

He had his steamboats, his railroad, his theaters, his carriages drawn
by six pure white horses, and his gorgeous girls, among whom was
Helen Josephine Mansfield.

He had set up his Josie in elegant quarters and showered her
with lavish gifts. After sundown of a trying day he would find
peace and exquisite joy at her ample bosom.

> *Croon me a lazy lullaby*
> *Let the lights burn low*
> *Wall Street smiles on men of might*
> *And weaklings dine on woe.*

His personal life was as fantastic as his career of plundering and
dragooning the markets. He made playthings of his gilded, luxurious
three-decker steamboats (one had a canary in each cabin), operated
by the Narragansett Company of which he became president in 1869.

Jim's greenish grey eyes would dance with joy as he stood at a
gangplank in full Admiral's uniform, a diamond blazing at his shirt
front, while gaping passengers blinked in wonder and admiration.
On occasion his darling of the hour stood beside him, correctly attired
in navy blue with brass buttons and epaulettes.

The high point in personal showmanship was reached when he
conveyed President Grant to Newport in one of his ships and then
accompanied him to Boston for the Peace Jubilee. There was an
orchestra of a thousand pieces at the coliseum. As he followed the
President down the aisle — a pompous glittering figure of an Admiral
— sixty thousand throats burst with cheers. Jubilee Jim smiled mod-
estly and took the bows.

There were people who said Fisk "wore his heart on his sleeve."
By some strange quirk he did indeed endear himself to a large part
of the public. This in spite of the thunders of the press, the outcries
of decent judges, and the continued withering blasts of Henry Ward
Beecher, who stormed: "A glaring meteor, abominable in his lusts,
and flagrant in his violation of public decency."

Perhaps the press was overdoing it. Americans have a queer
way of turning to the underdog. What if he did pay the bills of the
bankrupt Ninth Regiment to get himself elected Colonel and lead
moonlight parades up Fifth Avenue? And what if some people were
killed when Fisk and other officers lost their heads in the riot incident
to the Orangemen's parade? Still and all, wasn't he spending immense sums to provide opera?

French opera. The very words set his blood tingling. As an

impresario he began by rebuilding the Fifth Avenue Theater, which he managed, along with the Academy of Music. Then he spent nearly half a million dollars transforming the old Pike's Opera House into a glowing marble palace. From France he brought over entire troupes, and world famous conductors. In one spectacular success there was was a huge ballet; it was made up of blondes one night and brunettes the next. "Men like variety."

Never was Jim Fisk surrounded by so many lovely ladies. To him it was a dream come true. He adored them and they loved their handsome boss and fought for his favor. He even moved the Erie offices to the Opera building — sparkling offices that set a new high in commercial splendor.

Calm, tolerant Mrs. Fisk was enjoying the comforts of a long purse at her Newport villa; and the strikingly beautiful Josie Mansfield, who had accepted his bounty when she was down at the heel, was fading into the background. And the smouldering Josie knew it; she likewise knew of Jim's promiscuous escapades with the ladies from France.

Storm clouds broke and the lovers quarreled. Josie wanted more money, if not more attention. Jim grew angry and laid the facts on the line: He accused Josie of being unfaithful; he charged that his former friend, that socially prominent Adonis, Ned Stokes, with whom he had had dealings in oil, was spending his nights in Josie's arms.

Thus they parted, Jim with a heavy heart; and all his later pleading and gifts of money failed to regain her caresses.

Always a man of action, Mr. Fisk set out to destroy Ned Stokes. He pounded him in the courts, and had him arrested for alleged embezzlement, cancelled his Erie oil contracts, and otherwise bedeviled him until at length Josie hit back. For publication, she handed Stokes a packet of "sugar plum" love letters in which Fisk had poured out his amorous soul. Fisk bought them at a thumping big price, and at once charged the two with blackmail.

In a maze of suits and countersuits for libel and perjury the three principals marched through the courts like a miniature fashion parade. After a hearing on January 6, 1872, a rumor reached Stokes that he was to be indicted for blackmail.

Late that afternoon Mr. Fisk started up a side stairway of the Grand Central Hotel to call upon the daughter of a friend. He never reached the top. Two bullets — one in the arm and one in the abdomen — tumbled him over. A man running toward an exit was seized.

He was Ned Stokes. Before Fisk died seventeen hours later he iden-
tified Stokes as the one who had fired the shots.

After three trials, in which he pleaded self-defense, Stokes was
convicted of third degree manslaughter and served four years. Until
his death at sixty-one he always kept a light burning when he slept.
Critics said he feared Jim's ghost.

Jubilee Jim, the Prince of Erie, the King of Charlatans, was dead.
The news "rode on the winds" round the world. Soon a soft public
was slobbering over this "friend of the poor," even lauding his warm-
heartedness in badly written verse. Thousands crowded in to see the
resplendent Jim lying in state at the Opera House; other masses
packed Fifth Avenue as the cortege moved on its solemn way. Crowds
gathered in villages as the funeral train crawled to Brattleboro, where,
with extraordinary pomp, the happy hatchet man was buried — flowers in one hand, a military cap in the other.

Over the grave citizens placed an Italian marble monument cost-
ing twenty-five thousand dollars. At the massive base sit four marble
ladies, representing railroads, water traffic, commerce and, of course,
the stage.

Josie felt the icy chill of public disdain and sailed to Europe and
plied her trade at smart resorts. She kept her charm and astonished
the world in 1891 by marrying a rich American, brother of Viscountess
Falkland, Robert Livingston Reade, but the marriage was brief. She
returned, suffered a stroke, and was last recorded in 1901 seeking ad-
mittance to a Catholic Home in South Dakota.

5: Jay Gould : King Spider

Jay Gould loved flowers. He was an able botanist, an eager collector of orchids.

He also collected railroads and court injunctions. And when his colossal manipulations spread ruin and business paralysis he collected crowds beneath his window, angry crowds screaming for a lynching.

Yet he was a timid little man who asked only his pound of flesh and who, by overwork that killed him at fifty-six, collected seventy-two million dollars which he passed along to his children.

Brooding behind his mask of black whiskers he once sighed: "I am the most hated man in America." It was at a time when he was being called the Little Skunk of Wall Street, the Parasite of Disaster, and when the *New York Herald* was shouting: "It's always other persons' ill winds that do him the most good."

He seems to have had a miserable, somewhat sickly childhood on the little dairy farm of his father, John Burr Gould, at Roxbury, New York, where he was born on May 27, 1836. His grandfather, Abraham Gould, or Gold until 1806, had been one of the county's first settlers.

Young Jason Gould hungered for education, if only for the personal power it might give. But he quit school at fifteen, with a final composition headed, "Honesty is the Best Policy." Wrote his sister: "He did not engage in sports. In winter he would sometimes ride down once or twice on a sled. He was busy studying . . . geometry and logarithms, getting ready for surveying. He dreamed of building a railroad across the continent."

He became a crack surveyor, laboring with the intensity of the physically weak and embittered, and with a fanatic craving for wealth that was to make him a ruthless fighter and an astonishing buccaneer in an era of business and political rottenness.

From surveying and map-making he skipped to leather, and built up a large tannery business in Pennsylvania. Clouds of distrust soon

28

gathered; money records were confusing. His partner, who had put up the money, was glad to sell out to Charles Leupp, who in turn found accounts very confusing, and charged young Gould with speculating heavily in hides. And after the panic of 1857 Leupp went home one day and shot himself.

In a hectic battle over charges of fraud Gould was forced out, and went to New York, penniless, where he married the daughter of the wealthy grocer, Philip Miller.

It so happened that Mr. Miller had invested in a sixty-two mile railroad, the Rutland and Washington, then in final stages of decay, its stock worthless. He asked young Jay to look it over. In a short time Gould was President and Treasurer and soon sold the road to a connecting line for a profit of $130,000.

With this profit Gould got control of the battered Cleveland and Pittsburgh Railroad, juggled things about, and tripled his money by selling to the Pennsylvania Railroad.

At twenty-five he had arrived. He had the gambler's qualities without the gambler's two great faults — generosity and pity.

Up went a new sign on Wall Street in 1861: Smith, Gould and Martin, Brokers. Smith and Martin were active figures but not big time operators with inside information, so in the course of time Gould gradually pulled away from them and by the end of the Civil War had teamed up with Daniel Drew, Jim Fisk and other notorious stock jobbers.

There used to be a saying, "Don't get too close to Gould." Martin and Smith made this error. Martin became Gould's bitter enemy and died bankrupt in an asylum. Smith fought with Gould, went broke, and was forced from the Street.

In his voluminous testimony in courts and before Congressional Committees over spectacular freebooting in public lands, oil lands, coal lands (there were charges of appropriating assets, of perjury and violence) Gould always insisted he was in the railroad business.

This claim was justified, for he was involved in the operation or stock juggling, or both, of the Erie, where he served as President, the Missouri Pacific, Wabash, Union Pacific, Kansas Pacific, Denver Pacific, Texas Pacific, and the St. Louis and Northern. In 1880 he controlled ten thousand miles of track.

In these and numerous other enterprises, by his startling, hair-raising financial legerdemain he profited in panic and bankruptcy, piled millions on millions, sometimes broke his own companies while short-selling their stock, and ruined his friends with bland unconcern.

Once he testified on a giant manipulation: "I can't recall. I don't keep records. I carry everything in my head."

Strange indeed were the mental processes of busy, ingenious Mr. Gould, a man feared even by the mighty Cornelius Vanderbilt. In dull periods the Street knew "the Spider" was weaving new webs of receiverships, spurious stock issues and incredible bursts of inflation that rocked the money world.

Inventive and adroit were his many deals, including the greenback lock-up in 1868. It typified a propensity for original, detailed scheming. It was shocking and destructive and, in the words of the *Nation,* "the calmest spectator stands by in amazement and can only wonder when retribution will begin."

Gould fixed the pattern of his daring currency lock-up at a time when markets were booming. Money was easy, times were good, the business outlook bright, and the public was buying stocks on a broad scale. He figured, and correctly, that if interest rates suddenly could be shot skyward this would force heavy selling by the public and drive stock prices down. Thus a short-seller of stocks would profit.

Into the ruthless plot the intriguer brought tricky Jim Fisk and the aging Daniel Drew. Together they deposited in banks a total of $14,000,000, the largest share coming from Gould. Then they sold stocks short in huge volume.

In the meantime the banks, in the course of normal business, had made loans against these reserves and had put the deposited funds into circulation. Now the banks were in for a big surprise. For Gould and his associates appeared and requested certified checks for the entire amount of the deposits. Then they demanded greenbacks against these checks and proceeded to lock up the currency.

Of course the result was explosive. Banks were compelled to call their loans to brokers as a means of protecting their depleted reserves. Brokers in turn were forced to sell out customers who had borrowed on their stocks: Money rates had zoomed to 160 percent. An avalanche of stock liquidation sent prices down some thirty points.

It was a financial disaster. Trade in some parts of the country was brought to a standstill. Credit conditions were disrupted. Panic was beginning to spread across the land when, at the loud demands of business leaders, the United States Treasury stepped in and released enough reserve currency to lighten the strain. Action by Washington came none too soon, for banks were on the verge of suspension and the national credit was threatened.

Public indignation, deep and thunderous, had swelled to a point

where hard-crusted Daniel Drew had feared for his life and had
deserted Gould before the deal was over. For this timidity Gould
punished him soundly by skipping to the Bull side in time to catch
the old man "short" of Erie.

Outcries of ruined men, chorusing a threat to kill, rang in the
ears of quiet Mr. Gould after the deal was over and the profits
counted. He decided to remain at home for a few days with his
orchids, and his splendid art collection. His stable of fine horses and
carriages needed attention, and so did his yacht Atalanta.

Everything must be in proper order for bilious little Mr. Gould,
especially everything touching his private life, across which not the
slightest shadow was ever cast.

Shy and sensitive, particularly where family was concerned, yet
he seemed to feel no embarrassment for the family or for himself
when accused by the Hepburn investigating committee of taking
$12,000,000 from the Erie Treasury for himself, and of looting the
treasury in connection with the "India rubber" account. He could
always explain why Erie's capitalization was increased by some $60,-
000,000 in eight years: It was to keep the road out of the hands of
Vanderbilt.

As to that crowd of process servers frequently besieging his
offices, and as to the heavy guards present to protect these offices and
his life — well, any big business man "is likely to have some critics."

Shocking as it was in its consequences, the greenback lock-up
was but a prelude to the historic Gold Conspiracy which culminated
in Black Friday of September 24, 1869. Congress called it the most
shameless and revolting raid in the annals of organized speculation.

Soundness of national credit was based on the stability of paper
currency, known as greenbacks, and issued in the dark days of the
Civil War. A fall in greenbacks was the equivalent of a rise in gold.
This induced unbridled speculation in the yellow metal, first on the
Stock Exchange, from which it was banned for patriotic reasons, and
later in the new Gold Board at 24 Beaver Street.

In 1869 the Government held less than $100,000,000 in gold. The
floating market supply, on which speculation was based, totaled
about $20,000,000. Resourceful Mr. Gould reasoned that this supply
could be cornered, just as he cornered a stock. Hence those buying
gold for legitimate export purposes, and those short-selling gold for
speculation would be helplessly trapped. Success meant immense
profits.

There was one hitch. Gould must reach the President of the

United States and make sure the plot would not be wrecked by a sudden sale of gold by the Government.

So in late May of 1869 he paid a social visit to the aging Abel Corbin, lawyer, speculator and lobbyist, who recently had married Grant's sister, and who, supposedly, wielded strong influence over the President.

Corbin may have been impressed by the story that farm prosperity and industrial development required a higher price for gold. Or he may have had a single eye to the booty. In any case, Gould bought for his account $1,500,000 of gold at 133.

He also visited Grant at Corbin's home on June 15 during Grant's next trip to New York. Pushing the advantage he entertained the naive Grant in a private box at Jim Fisk's theater and took him to Newport on the Fisk yacht with other speculators, including Cyrus W. Field, a former rag dealer, who laid the first Atlantic cable, became a Wall Street tycoon, and lived out his last years on charity.

On the subject of gold Grant was noncommittal — "a wet blanket" — but from June to August Gould bought gold stealthily and heavily. To buttress his campaign he had imposing analyses prepared by an English expert showing the need of higher gold prices. Widely published, these articles were brought to Grant's attention by innumerable visitors, many of them secret emissaries of Gould.

Glad tidings came on September 2. Corbin told Gould that Grant had instructed Secretary of the Treasury Boutwell to sell no gold without specific instructions. Now the trap was set. The price of gold, 130 when Gould started buying, soon leaped to 137. Corbin received a token check on profits — made in blank — for $25,000; Gould bought for General Butterfield, Assistant Treasurer at New York, a Corbin man, $1,500,000 of gold, and proposed a purchase for General Horace Porter, Grant's secretary, who promptly squelched the move.

At this point Fisk was drawn into the deal. He was suspicious: "Says I, 'the deal isn't air-tight.'" Fisk wanted more assurance of Grant's position. So the little black-whiskered man did a reckless thing. He sent a special messenger to Grant with a note urging no sales of gold under any condition. General Porter opened the note, promptly unburdened his suspicions, and prevailed upon Grant to end Corbin's tie-up with Gould.

At once Mrs. Grant wrote Mrs. Corbin that the President was upset over ugly rumors concerning Corbin. Fear struck Corbin's heart. He showed the letter to Gould, flatly withdrew from the plot, and asked for his $100,000 paper profit. A check was written but never delivered.

Gould wiggled and stalled. Here indeed was a kettle of fish. If the letter's contents became known — the fact that White House "protection" was gone — ruin was certain, for Gould was saddled with $100,000,000 of gold and the prospect of a collapsing market. He had in fact built his own trap.

So he built a bigger trap. He asked Fisk to go onto the Exchange and bid gold up to 160 no matter how much he had to buy. "But give only verbal orders, no written ones." Like a wild bull Fisk rushed onto the floor next morning. With his chief brokers, Albert Speyer and William Belden, he jacked up the price amid scenes of riotous confusion. By day's end Gould had craftily sold all his gold at top prices — mostly to Fisk and his brokers.

Not one word did Gould utter at that night's strategy confab; nor at the stormy session next day, Black Friday, when he sat huddled in a corner of the Gold Room, quiet and calm, directing things by an occasional nod, and at critical times tearing off the corners of a newspaper.

Sleepless crowds had gathered early. They had spilled out of the Gold Room into nearby streets by the time blustering Jim Fisk swept upon the floor like a cyclone. "150! 155! 160!" he bellowed. Half a million went at 160. "161 for five million!" he shouted defiantly, "162 for five million!"

Said the quiet voice of James Brown, a Scottish banker: "Sold at 162." There was a moment of stunned silence. "Then hell broke loose." The government was selling gold; the bubble had burst, and the room became a shouting, cursing, struggling mob.

Amid threats to shoot the Gould clique, Broker Speyer went mad, leaped to a chair, shouting: "Shoot me! Shoot me!" He was carried off hatless, coatless, screaming: "I bid 180!"

On that Black Friday hundreds of firms collapsed, thousands of men were ruined, half of Wall Street was bankrupt, and the Gold Room closed for good.

In a hack, with blinds drawn, Gould and Fisk escaped to the safety of their Erie stronghold, where Gould heard cries under his window: "Who killed Leupp? . . . Lynch! Lynch!"

Why the big hands of Jim Fisk did not close on the hairy little throat in the hack for the double-cross is a perpetual riddle. Doubtless Gould revealed his settlement plan quickly. It was this. Fisk would repudiate all purchases by his brokers, Speyer and Belden, who had acted only on verbal orders. They in turn would accept the purchases and declare themselves bankrupt. Gould would give each an income for life, and take care of Fisk.

And why not? Gould's profit was $11,000,000. His debit "an enduring reputation for diabolic evil." Said Jim Fisk: "Let everyone carry out his own corpse."

After much fumbling by controlled judges, the matter reached Congress, as all things do. There were protracted breast-beating investigations, and then the subject was quietly buried. Fisk testified to his anger at the bungling Corbin: "Says I, 'you damned old scoundrel . . .'" But even Fisk could not slug a pious, doddering rascal in his own home.

Mr. Gould turned his attention back to his lands and his forests and his railroads, particularly to the Erie which he continued to milk until, in righteous horror, the stockholders charged him with channeling $12,803,059 to his own account. To escape criminal charges he agreed to turn over certain buildings and also stocks to the par value of $6,000,000, which stocks, incidentally, were later found to be worth but $200,000. Finally, in 1874, he bowed and parted with Erie, the Scarlet Woman of Wall Street.

As the years flowed along there were more frequent bilious attacks, insomnia, and then weakness of the lungs, and on December 2, 1892, the swarthy little man with the black whiskers entered the windowless house of death.

Wall Street is realistic. Wall Street danced with joy. Stocks went up.

6: Long Shadows

Great private fortunes had their impact upon the course of history, sometimes good, sometimes bad.

There was a day when each feudal noble set up his own means of exchange; if the castle sought new profit it was a simple process to debase the bullion or local coinage.

Out of a deep financial morass the Republic of Florence in 1252 first undertook continuous gold coinage. It marked the surge of the Renaissance toward money and luxury. Nowhere was the new spirit so vigorous as in Florence, and the highest Florentine exemplars were the Medici.

It was the Medici who set the course characteristic of high finance. Their operations began in trade, moved on into banking, and spread out over a wider and wider range until they included governmental adventures. History shows that it is difficult to achieve large financial stature without involvement in politics, for governments want money, and money is known to have influenced government. The middle-class Medici family were founders of a commercial aristocracy which, centuries later, was to wrest financial supremacy from the crown coffers of Europe. But like many other seekers of great permanent wealth, the Medici stumbled, and in the course of time the treasure of the family faded.

Again on the pages of financial history may be found the bold story of the Fuggers, the Austrian financial backers of the Habsburgs Son of a weaver and trader, Jakob Fugger II, born in 1459, with his nephew pyramided a trading fortune by lending money to the vain and ambitious Habsburgs on the security of Tyrolese silver and copper mines and the revenues of land holdings. With repeated Habsburg defaults, these prizes fell, one by one, to the Fuggers.

Jakob regarded himself as a benefactor of society, even when he engineered one Habsburg's election as King of the Romans by putting up the traditional bribes for the Electors, but already the public thought of him as a dangerous monopolist. He moved on into Spanish business, leasing from the crown the revenues of three great ecclesiastical orders, and died in the happy thought that in his last fifteen years the family fortune had shown a 900 percent profit.

Nephew Anton Fugger carried on, financing another Habsburg's election as King of Rome and heaped wealth on wealth, until a day came when Saxony and France clashed with the Habsburgs, and this was the beginning of ultimate disaster. When Anton died in 1560, chief assets of the house were claims against Spain for four million florins. As the years ticked off the once giant fortune of the Fuggers consisted only of parcels of heavily mortgaged lands, reminders to a scattered family of a golden age that was gone.

Then there was Jacques Coeur, born in 1395, a trader of Bourges, who organized the French markets dealing with the Levant. He freed them from Venetian, Genoese and Florentine control. His sprawling business included mines, paper and silk mills, and a big commercial fleet, and his traffic was approved both by the Pope and the Sultan of Egypt.

France went bankrupt in a defensive war when the English seized a substantial part of northwestern France, including Paris and Reims. Coeur leaped to the rescue of Charles VII when no more funds could be raised from the nobility. Coeur advanced a sum more than a fifth of the throne's total revenues, and outfitted the winning armies. For this he was ennobled and made the new overseer of the finances of France.

But there were lady troubles ahead. When in 1449 the King's mistress, Agnes Sorel, was brought to bed in childbirth and died, Coeur was accused by certain courtiers of giving her poison. He was tried and convicted, not of murder but of sharp business practices and of traffic with the infidel Sultan. Coeur escaped to Rome where he died a year later, and his great estate was scattered and evaporated.

Richelieu, the French Prime Minister, once referred to the Baring Brothers as the sixth great European power. They typified the link between immense private fortunes and governments of modern Europe.

Two sons of a wool manufacturer founded the house of Baring in 1770 and in two decades its tentacles reached deep into the hearts of governments. Francis, the younger brother, was Governor of the East India Company. His son bought great tracts of land in Maine and Pennsylvania, and married the daughter of Senator William Bingham of Philadelphia, then rated the richest man in the States.

Their gigantic transactions included the indemnity loan granted to France after its defeat by Wellington; they were able in 1839 to shore up the Bank of England, and in 1847 the Banque de France. But when Argentina defaulted in 1890 on huge loans for speculative expansion the historic house of Baring was saved only by the combined efforts of the governments of England and France. Its influence on governments was largely at an end.

The powerful Rothschild family who gained wealth by betting against Napoleon and whose private banking system formed a network over Europe watched their star pale in the shifting tides of politics and economy. By the end of World War I their day of glory was little more than a memory.

In the Orient the gigantic Mitsui family firm symbolized the flowering of private finance. Before World War II the firm, whose interests embraced stores, manufacturing, and banking, controlled 15 percent of the entire capital investment of Japan and 20 percent of the empire's foreign trade. In 1946 the Mitsuis voted their family council out of existence.

Thus does time take its toll of concentrated private wealth.

Most great fortunes in the earlier days of America were built on speculation. In fact, America itself was a speculation — a speculation to Columbus, and a speculation to the kings of Spain and France and England, who viewed it as a source of riches in gold and silver and pelts.

Kings gave vast tracts of land to favorites and to companies as royal rewards. Out of the custom grew a cycle of land grabbing and town jobbing.

Colonial land grabbing was indulged in by Washington, Franklin, Patrick Henry and other leading Americans of the day. But it was a mere prelude in the epic of land speculation which, after the revolution, broke out with violence and sustained fury.

Thus booms and collapses were inevitable and, incidentally, they were occurring before a stock exchange was present to register the peaks and valleys, but perhaps with somewhat less frequency.

The first general speculative frenzy by the American public occurred in the Civil War period. Women traded in gold; men of the church liked mining and oil stocks. Lawyers, who are notori-

ously bad speculators, preferred Erie, for the Scarlet Lady was never
dull. Merchants centered on commodities.

A tooth and claw economic age unfolded in broad panorama
from the Civil War until the end of the century, and it spawned a
class of men of volcanic energy and immense courage. They swept
into power and dominated the business and financial machinery, the
banks and the exchanges. They were called empire builders, kings
of commerce, and sometimes more colorful names.

These men of strong will and unbridled imagination arrived on
the scene when America was an agrarian-mercantile democracy; they
transformed it into a unified industrial economy. Under the drive of
such men — Jay Cooke, Vanderbilt, Carnegie, Rockefeller, Morgan,
Hill and Harriman — the industrial revolution swept onward, broadscale production displaced scattered, local, decentralized production,
and waste gave way to efficiency. The giants who had seized economic power built up the nation, sometimes at the cost and suffering
of the people, who cried out against the wrongs committed.

America was fully prepared for the industrial revolution. Watt's
steam engine and Stephenson's locomotive, both brought from England,
had been quickly refined by Yankee genius. A new era of navigation
had opened up when Fulton put the engine in a ship; in four years
steamboats were plying the Mississippi. The West and the Eastern
seaboard had been linked by the Erie Canal. John Deere's shiny steel
plow had cut the rich prairies of the West, and McCormick had
fashioned a revolutionary reaper; people followed wheat from Chicago to Puget Sound. Morse had invented the telegraph, a mighty
instrument of commerce that knit the nation into one big business
family.

Rail shares were a basis of speculation almost from July 4, 1828,
when Charles Carroll, signer of the Declaration of Independence,
laid the cornerstone of the first road, the Baltimore and Ohio. Rails
needed broad national financing. Such business flowed to New York
banks; private banks grew up to give securities wide distribution;
volume grew on the New York Stock Exchange, and Wall Street became undisputed money center of the land.

Jacob Little, a new type of manipulator who arrived on the scene
in the early era of rail development, was an uncompromising bear
who thrived on disaster and who, like Drew, Fisk, Gould and others,
cast long shadows over Wall Street and implanted suspicion and distrust in the public mind.

It was the ingenious Little who invented the short sale, and so

fierce was his passion for bearish speculation that all else was shut
from his life. He heaped destruction upon destruction until he was
hated by the pack; three times their combined onslaughts sent him
spinning into bankruptcy. The fourth time he was destroyed, failing
for $10,000,000, and carrying various firms down with him. Bad as
speculation was, cruel and ruthless as it was, the preponderance of
sentiment was not on Little's side — the short-seller's side — but on
the bull side, the optimistic side, the side of American growth and
progress.

Oddly enough, most of the big operators of the Jacob Little era,
a class of men just below the titans of great outside wealth and manipulative genius, died bankrupt, or at least in circumstances far from
affluence.

Brilliant Leonard W. Jerome, lawyer, editor, Consul at Trieste,
turned his talents to Wall Street and ran a shoestring five hundred
dollars into a quick fortune. He formed a brokerage firm with
William R. Travers, and handled big market deals for Vanderbilt,
piling up gains for himself and his brother Addison who, incidentally,
made three million dollars in his first nine months on Wall Street.

Then, while Leonard was in Europe, Addison Jerome tried a
daring rail corner against the astute Henry Keep, lost his millions
and died.

Leonard Jerome husbanded his fortune with greater discretion
but, even so, in the course of years he involved himself in a Pacific
Mail corner and was cleaned out, save for a few parcels of real
estate. Wisely he turned his back on Wall Street and lived out his
days in Paris.

Anthony Morse had his day of glory, piling one rail manipulation upon another until a dark hour when he failed and carried a
score of firms down with him — at the very time, curiously, when
Vanderbilt, with his greater millions, was pushing a Harlem Railroad
corner to success in the teeth of an adverse market trend.

Market trends could and did pauperize clever and famous speculators, such as William H. Marston; they had less effect upon August
Belmont, Henry Keep, John Tobin and the Schell brothers.

Mining millionaires of the West could toy with Wall Street and
convulse markets, regardless of trends, without endangering their
basic wealth. Some of these men were only incidentally associated
with The Street, such as John W. Mackay (later Mackay telegraph),
James Flood, W. S. O'Brien, and James G. Fair, who pooled their

funds and gained high wealth from the Comstock Lode mine. Three of them had been bartenders.

Others who churned the markets with splendid disdain of public rights had made their millions in Far West rail building, including Collis Huntington, Mark Hopkins, Darius Mills and Leland Stanford. All helped to deepen the shadows of distrust that stretched down the years.

Streaking westward in the two decades up to 1880, iron rails spanned the continent amid an upsurge of public speculation that touched dizzy heights. Roads were badly planned, launched in fits of optimism, and almost invariably badly financed. As Vanderbilt lamented just before the historic Jay Cooke collapse in 1873, they were "buildng railroads from nowhere to nowhere at public expense. . . ."

Vanderbilt should have known, for he had picked up his share of railroads before he died at eighty-three, leaving a hundred million dollars as a monument to his almost unnatural gift of prophesy.

By reason of a glowing reputation in handling government fiscal engagements, it had been a simple task for Jay Cooke and Company to spread stock of the huge Northern Pacific Railroad project among the wealthy and humble alike. Before completion, however, the Franco-Prussian war burst out and the European syndicates promptly cancelled enormous subscriptions.

At about this time new scandals in Wall Street sent money rates sky high; a panicky public began selling. Thereupon Cooke poured his own company funds into the big enterprise to keep construction going, only to topple shortly in a sensational failure that carried along scores of banks and commercial enterprises in the panic of 1873. Another long shadow was cast over Wall Street.

Licking its deep wounds, the money lane lay quiet for some time before regaining balance and confidence. As always, new talent leaped into leadership. There was, for instance, such men as the colorful James R. Keene, English born lawyer and mine expert. He ran a handful of cheap mining shares into $200,000; then he reversed his position and pyramided short sales into a $13,000,000 nest egg. He became a power in Wall Street, scaling ever higher barriers, until finally Jay Gould got bored with him and put him back where he had started.

Then there was Henry Villard, the stock waterer, who multiplied his rail promotions into lofty wealth — even into control of the Northern Pacific — and who later thinned his speculations into vulnerability and was clipped with terrible finality. He stayed far from the Street with his meager remaining funds.

Right on top of this quake came a far more sensational and disastrous stroke in the failure of Ward and Grant, a firm in which former President Grant was a special partner. For sheer cussedness and financial trickery this affair, sparked by one Ferdinand Ward, has few parallels in history.

Able, scheming son of a minister, Ward had worked hard in Wall Street for a stake. In the course of time his spectacular fireworks in rail shares lighted the financial skies. He came to be called a "young Napoleon."

Grant's rather dull son had to his credit only a rich marriage; of business he knew even less than his naive father. Ward deftly snared the name of Grant for his unscrupulous and incredible operations. Young Grant invested a substantial sum in the firm, and then his father was beguiled into tossing in his own fortune and becoming a special partner.

Nor were they alone. Ward's curious brand of optimism engulfed the respected James D. Fish, president of the Marine National Bank, whose resources, in the end, were being diverted to the conspiracy in violation of the law.

Into the "investment" scheme were drawn rich and poor alike. Shorn of its trimmings, Ward's racket consisted of paying ridiculously large returns to investors out of the money they themselves had put up. He juggled the books to cover huge speculative drives that had failed.

Happy in their plush offices, their fool's paradise, the Grants signed without question and without even reading, all papers shoved before them by the genius. That is, until May 7, 1884, when the Marine bank tumbled under the strain, and then down came the Metropolitan Bank, and then Ward and Grant. Thus was touched off the panic of 1884.

Ward and Grant failed for $16,000,000 at a time when Ward's spurious records showed assets of nearly twice that amount. Thousands of people, investors and depositors, saw their life savings wiped out and were reduced to poverty, as indeed was Grant himself. Humiliated, embittered, broken in health, he died a year later.

Ward got off with ten years in prison, Fish with seven. In those days sin lay in getting caught.

Wall Street, like the whole country, was bursting at the seams.

No longer could one man lead the speculative orchestra into a sooth-ing lullaby, such as had gladdened the shriveled heart of old Daniel Drew and brought joy to the amorous soul of Jubilee Jim Fisk.

Rail manipulators of the early expansion period were forced to give way to railroad magnates and consolidators, such as James J. Hill and E. H. Harriman, men of constructive viewpoint. Into the spotlight came oil barons, John D. Rockefeller, H. M. Flagler, Charles Pratt and Henry H. Rogers. Their developments fired the public imagination.

So, too, did the rise of the steel industry under the terrific drive of Andrew Carnegie, H. C. Frick and Charles M. Schwab, a drive that in 1901 brought creation of the United States Steel Corporation, a super-trust, dazzling in its immensity.

In the exciting trust building period, which brought on enact-ment of the Sherman Anti-Trust Act in 1890 — a law that lay dor-mant for the next decade — such men as J. P. Morgan and Jacob H. Schiff, greatly influenced banking and finance.

Most of the industrial consolidation was sound and logical and in the public interest. But the period afforded golden opportunity to tricksters who promoted sham projects and flooded the markets with watered stock. These promotions helped to bring on the panic of 1893, which was aided, too, by the government's unsound infla-tionary money policy.

Two incidents helped to touch off this panic. Philadelphia & Reading Railroad sought to set up a nationwide rail combination against the wishes of the Morgan and Vanderbilt interests. The re-sulting crash in Reading stock was devastating.

National Cordage Company, a typical watered-stock promotion, toppled at a cost of $20,000,000 to the public. Thirteen brokerage houses went down, and subsequent failures included 642 banks and 15,000 commercial companies.

In time a new bull market developed, the McKinley bull market, which was permitted to go gaily on its way until 1903. Then acute indigestion, occasioned by flotation of too many issues of good and bad stock, brought a new collapse that carried down another string of brokerage houses.

Wall Street's power had been tremendously enhanced by the astonishing growth of the Standard Oil empire, created by John D. Rockefeller. He had moved his headquarters from Cleveland to the New York money center in 1882, and thereafter his nod carried great weight. In creation of his giant oil industry we see again the familiar

pattern of good and evil. While most of the Rockefeller expansion
methods were bad from the present-day viewpoint, the indisputable
facts are that benefits to mankind were almost beyond measure.

Like Rockefeller, James J. Hill was a builder. He was born on
a Canadian farm September 16, 1838, and when he was sixteen years
old he started on a trip to the east. At St. Paul he missed the packet;
instead of loafing for a month he went to work for a river shipping
agent.

Soon his inquisitive mind had encompassed transportation problems and he set up in business for himself. A few failures studded
his record of successes, but he never lacked backing, for he inspired
confidence among the people in the thinly-settled northwest.

With Norman Kittson he launched a steamer-rail-stage line for
freight and passengers from St. Paul to Winnipeg. At Winnipeg they
met Donald A. Smith, later Lord Strathcona, Canadian railroad king.
The three men saw eye to eye, consummated a number of large deals,
and in the course of time obtained control of the tottering St. Paul
and Pacific Railroad, "two streaks of rust," a sorry road trying to com-
pete with the mighty Northern Pacific. Their success was phenomenal.

Hill's genius touched the heights in population development, in
accelerating emigration into the northwest through free excursions
and other inducements to settlers, and in time he became known as
an Empire Builder. Under his touch raw prairies were transformed
into rich farms and thriving villages and towns. Settlers adored him,
gloried in his wealth and power, and rejoiced when, with Morgan
backing, he was able to snatch control of the northwest's two giant
roads — the Great Northern Railroad and the Northern Pacific.

Complete success had been achieved by 1893; but ahead lay a
test of continued power, a Wall Street battle of historic proportions
against another genius named Edward Henry Harriman.

Son of a clergyman and ten years Hill's junior, Harriman started
out as an office boy at fourteen and remained in Wall Street all his
life. At twenty-two he launched his own brokerage business, frequently served Gould and Vanderbilt, and then tried a few stock
manipulations on his own. The results were bad.

Rails definitely were his field. His first deal involved purchase
and sale of a small road at a big profit. In that deal he discovered a
formula; it was to pick up one small but strategic road after another,

get the big lines to fighting over control, and then at the peak of battle unload to the top bidder.

With his fortune swelling (he had gained control of Illinois Central Railroad) Harriman fought the Union Pacific reorganization plan of Kuhn, Loeb and Company until in desperation they conceded to him a block of stock and a directorship; by 1900 he was that road's controlling factor.

Hill frowned upon the increasing competition of Union Pacific under Harriman leadership and decided to buy the Chicago, Burlington & Quincy to allow his Northern Pacific a terminus in Chicago. Harriman, too, wanted Burlington because as a parallel road it was a threat to Union Pacific traffic. The giants met in a battle of money bags, which became another spectacle of unbridled manipulative effort that shook Wall Street. In the end Hill was victorious; but the really big war still lay ahead.

And it was not long in coming. It grew into the most gigantic open market struggle staged in Wall Street for corporate control. Backed by Kuhn-Loeb millions, Harriman set out to wrest control of Northern Pacific from Hill, who was backed by the Morgan millions. In two months, beginning in March of 1901 Harriman succeeded in buying up a majority of the preferred stock, but not quite a majority of the common. Nonetheless, success seemed certain.

Shocked by developments, Morgan cabled from England, directing the purchase of 150,000 shares of Northern Pacific common stock in the open market to safeguard the Hill-Morgan margin of control. This buying shot the price up from 112 to 149.

A condition in the Northern Pacific charter permitted redemption of the preferred by action of the directors on any January 1. Morgan and Hill thereupon ordered that such steps be taken to further strengthen their position.

Meantime turmoil swept the Exchange, the Street and the entire business world. The titanic struggle had brought about a complete corner on May 8, 1901. Hundreds of shorts were hopelessly trapped. They began unloading other stocks in a tidal wave of selling; they needed cash to cover their short sales in Northern Pacific. Call money sky-rocketed to seventy percent.

While conservative securities were crashing from thirty to eighty points, Northern Pacific common leaped upward ten, twenty, and finally fifty points at a crack until it touched a top of a thousand dollars a share. New terror raced across the business world — a dread fear of panic, with a cyclone of failures.

This fear struck anxiety into the hearts of the Kuhn-Loebs, the Jacob Schiffs, the Harrimans, Hills and Morgans. After all, their own priceless enterprises were being dumped on the auction block of panic.

So these realistic men did a very practical thing. They got together and let the shorts settle, not at a thousand dollars a share, but at $150 a share. Then they formed a holding company, the Northern Securities Company, for the stocks of all the roads controlled by both sides. Each of the two groups was given equal representation on the board. Pleasantly they sat down together, disposed of the amenities, and then talked in serious tones of the golden future, the greater and broader destiny of a restless and dynamic land, driven onward by restless, dynamic men. Bygones were bygones.

Giants ruled supreme in industry and finance at the turn of the century. It was frequently charged, in and out of Congress, that twelve men held complete control; these men, it was claimed, regarded themselves as benevolent despots chosen to develop the country as suited their convenience.

Whatever the facts, the leaders were less crude than those of the Jay Gould type of a preceding generation. For one thing lawyers had found the tooth and claw methods distasteful and increasingly dangerous from a legal standpoint.

But no deep consciousness of public rights had developed in creating the new giant industries, and the case of steel was no exception. Here a group of adventurous pioneers had swung into action after Henry Bessemer had found a method of freeing iron of its impurities. Andrew Carnegie captained the hardy group who became known as the Pittsburgh millionaires, and his empire became the nucleus of the United States Steel Corporation. Wall Street provided the machinery; stock was deftly distributed to the public, and many men of modest means who bought it and kept it grew rich as a consequence of their faith in the new giant.

Formation of the big steel corporation typified the ultimate rulership of J. Pierpont Morgan over the moneyed aristocracy of America. He was the first banker capable of snatching railroad and other corporate control from the speculators and promoters.

More and more the Street's big banking houses, and not individuals, took leadership in the huge consolidations, in the mergers of metals and mines, farm tools, tobaccos and motors, and each amalgamation added to the power of The Street.

But one captain of industry who never stood, hat in hand, at the feet of the money giants was Henry Ford. At the very outset he determined to have no part of any enterprise controlled or directed by bankers. He would finance his business out of earnings, and this he did after a few false starts, and in subsequent decades he left Wall Street drooling for a cut in his remarkable success.

While William C. Durant, one of Wall Street's most rash and resourceful promoters, moved in and out of control of General Motors, with his dreams of ever greater conquests, and while other captains of the motorcar industry cast their lots with the New York money lane, Ford held aloof and his empire rose steadily in magnitude. His unique achievement shines out in the astonishing record of Twentieth Century industrial expansion. The new $238,000,000 Ford Foundation is additional evidence of his contribution to society.

Ford stood alone, and aside, in complete control of his own great properties, untouched by the broad public speculation in other motor shares which added so tremendously to the volume of transactions as well as to the growth of the New York Stock Exchange, right up to the historic crash in 1929, a crash that deeply influenced the political trend of a nation.

7: Cornelius Vanderbilt : Ships and Rails

Wall Street historians, quick to stress the shadowy aspects of the Vanderbilt saga, often leave in wretched unbalance the Commodore's mighty achievements, his monumental contributions to the nation's industrial expansion.

Granting that his aims were selfish, that he was a tough little number even at six who could ride bareback and win races, and at twelve did a man's labor to escape school — "will ye hark the little devil cuss, and the milk not dry on his lips" — and even allowing for the hundred million dollars he piled up for himself, the end results nonetheless clearly proved his singular greatness as a builder.

He was indeed as hard as the cruel and ruthless business era in which he lived; as rugged physically as the family of poor Dutch farmers named van der Bilt who came from Holland to the colony of New Netherlands sometime after the middle of the seventeenth century. Honest, sturdy, hard-working, they lived always on the edge of want, reared huge families, and somehow wrenched a home from the wilderness.

Vanderbilt's father, a slow, unimaginative plodder who farmed and ran a ferry with equal mediocrity, was fortunate in his marriage to Phebe Hand, a strong, buxom, moderately well-educated girl of a higher social strata, the niece of Major-general Edward Hand who distinguished himself in the Revolution.

To Phebe Hand, a woman of great heart and high spirit, a fourth child and second son was born May 27, 1794, a lusty deep-chested brat who was named Cornelius for his father. Like this father, as he grew toward adolescence, he was big-bodied, rangy, blue-eyed and tow-headed — the surface marks of a Dutchman. But his mother's English blood showed in his features and in his character. He had her square chin and jaw, her sweep of brow, her humorous glint of the eyes, and best of all her mingling of foresight and determination

47

which carried him through the struggles of a dramatic life.

This foresight of the mother surged yeastily in the soul of the son. He became one of those rare men gifted with an extra sense, a sense that enabled him to comprehend the trends of the future; he drove forward, always deaf to the turmoil about him, toward horizons unseen by ordinary eyes.

From childhood young Corneel had paid his own way by odd jobs. By the time he was ten he had cussed and scuffed his way to leadership among neighborhood boys, who frequently were snared into helping with his work long before Tom Sawyer was born, and he was also making trips in his father's periauger, a harbor boat, sitting square and confident, a firm hand on the tiller, an eye on the main sheet.

Even at this tender age he deplored his father's inefficiency, his irregularity of ferry trips that lost business; and his father, in turn, was suspicious of the boy's electric energy, his eager aggressiveness. They didn't get on well. So some years later young Corneel, watching the freighters with ballooned sails nose into harbor, decided to run away to sea.

But first he must consult his mother, as he did on most important matters all of her long life. While the youngest of Phebe's nine children nursed at her breast she listened patiently to his story, then gave the verdict: "Corneel, I jest won't have you go to sea, not with my goodwill. I need you, son."

Crestfallen, the lad made a new attempt: "Ma, if I only had my own boat I could make more'n Pa right now. There's good money in the harbor. I could give you a sight more'n I do now."

Phebe was convinced. Somehow she scraped up the hundred dollars for a periauger on condition that he plow and sow an eight-acre rocky field by his sixteenth birthday, then only twenty-seven days off. He drew other boys into the work on the promise of free moonlight rides, and on the morning of his birthday the task had been done, he had his twenty-passenger boat, and the astonishing Vanderbilt career was launched.

Boys living in the present age of golden opportunity, whining for parental help, or boasting of unemployment checks, might well study the life of young Vanderbilt, the boatman, who, without benefit of wage-and-hour laws or child labor statutes, through sheer grit and frugality acquired three thousand dollars in three years. And until he was of age he gave his parents all of his day and half of his night earnings.

When he started his ferry service between Whitehall Landing and Staten Island, New York was a sprawling country town with pleasant tree-lined streets. Above City Hall were fields and pasture lands.

After two years, the war of 1812 deadened the harbor trade, but in the Bay the men-of-war needed boat service, as did garrisons at the forts. By 1814 we find the "hustling Vanderbilt boy" under contract for supplying the posts in the lower harbor with one load a week each. On this task he spent most of his nights; his day-time ferry service kept to schedule. Sunday was his day of sleep.

Money began pouring in, lots of it; he had married his cousin, Sophia Johnson, in 1813, and next year built a schooner, the Dread, and followed this with a trim, swift coasting vessel called the Charlotte, sailing them up and down the coast as far south as Charleston. By his twenty-fourth birthday he was the owner of several sailing vessels and nine thousand dollars in cash and his position as a harbor boatman was solidly established. Then he did one of those extraordinary things, so typical of the Vanderbilt career:

"Ma, I'm goin' to sell all my boats. . . . I see steamboats comin' to the rivers and bays. B'ilers have it over sails, Ma." Phebe didn't protest; nor did she comment when friends said he was plumb crazy to toss aside a fine business and take a job as steamboat captain at a thousand dollars a year. She understood. She and her son had vision.

So Captain Corneel went to work for William Gibbons, owner of the New York-Brunswick ferry line, guiding the snorting, cranky little Stoughtenger up and down the water lane and ignoring the jibes at this "Mouse - of - the - Mountain" which was propelled by groaning "palmipedes" to get around the Fulton-Livingston monopoly on side wheels.

A condition bordering on anarchy prevailed, for there was as yet no Federal jurisdiction over navigable waterways. In granting the monopoly New York state had entered into controversies with all neighboring states, blocking progress and improvement — creating a stage set to order for the fiery young crusader.

Wars of competition flared continuously during his ten years with Gibbons; they were intensified when the Bellona appeared with side wheels, and when still other Gibbons boats were added, all built to the Vanderbilt specifications. Subpoena servers hung around the hotel in New Brunswick where Vanderbilt lived, once a fleebag leased to him rent free by Gibbons, and which his wife had transformed into a clean, profitable tavern, a highlight in her rather drab and lonely married life.

Injunctions, seizures and law suits marched down these strenuous years; often Captain Corneel dropped his crew in New Jersey and brought the Bellona alone to her New York wharf and slept in a secret closet in the hold while angry process servers stormed the deck in vain. Sometimes his cold eyes and craggy, forbidding face were enough to scare them off; again he tricked them into arresting him without cause, and loud guffaws echoed up and down the river: "That Corneel, he's a smart young bastard," boatmen would say in rising admiration.

He was indeed smart enough to learn everything about steamboating, just as he had set out to do. And while learning, he made money for Gibbons, enough money so that Gibbons could engage the brilliant Daniel Webster to fight the monopoly. And Chief Justice Marshall finally held with Webster. The monopoly was smashed in 1824 in a major decision that helped cement the union of the states, a decision whose effect on commerce was electric; in the ensuing five years the nation raced forward with unprecedented speed.

Strange as it may seem, the name of Vanderbilt, a name synonomous with great wealth often questionably employed, bobs up frequently on the side of progress and the general good. In common fairness he must be given much credit for the crushing of the monopoly and the lifting of an iron curtain against progress.

Victory called for new fields to conquer. In his coming battles he wanted a free hand. Gibbons almost wept when Captain Corneel decided to go into business for himself, refusing a proffered half interest in the Gibbons lines. He bought the Bellona in 1828, and next year built his first ship, the Citizen; then followed other craft, one by one, and soon Corneel was in the thick of battle with powerful owners who ganged up to drive him off the Hudson. But he thrived on such wars with the "interests" and fashioned favorable compromises which disposed of the North River Association, the Peekskill route of Daniel Drew, and others, each in its turn. At length it dawned on the trade that naught was gained in battles with this steely-eyed man of destiny. So the Hudson crowd let him alone, let him build up his magnificent fleet of fifty odd boats which plied the river for three decades.

Events were moving rapidly. Democracy, a raw, blatant, cocksure democracy, was on the march, kicking aside conservative busi-

ness methods inherited from the mother country, building, speculating, pyramiding profits; government, business and economics set the
pattern, and hard-boiled old Andrew Jackson typified the age. Booms
and panics in stark succession were enough to sink the democracy,
but after each calamity it rose up and drove to greater heights.

Each economic stride found Vanderbilt up front in the pageant;
as in 1836 when on June 13 history was made by the Novelty which
steamed up the Hudson from New York to Albany, dead against the
tide, in a breath-taking twelve hours. It was burning anthracite coal,
with watertube boilers invented by Dr. Elijah Nott, President of
Union College. Coal cost: $100, as against $240 for the wood previously consumed. Saving for a season in operating the Novelty,
$19,000. So "Black rocks" replaced wood in steamships, the coal
industry boomed, water traffic soared, and trade was revivified.

No one was quicker than Corneel to realize the implications of
the new era of coal, and in that year he doubled his income and was
listed with the city's sixteen rich men, though politely passed up by
Society as a rough uncultured fellow.

Like a fanatic he fought on, weaving his web of lines covering
Long Island Sound and the rich New England ports. He kept regular
schedules to Bridgeport, Norwalk, Derby, New Haven, Hartford,
Providence and Boston. Now he was rich enough to test his ideas.
Under the spell of his restless energy river and Sound steamers became larger and faster, with sumptuous staterooms and glittering
salons. And all the time his bitter, incredible competition kept
driving down travel costs. By 1840 he would carry a passenger from
New York to Albany for $2, a distance of 150 miles. Dinner and
breakfast included.

To add zest to the vicious competition, Vanderbilt's proud vessels
were pitted in races against those of opposing lines, sometimes with
big side bets; boiler room machinery was wrecked in these contests,
some of which were lost, even with Corneel himself at the wheel.
The celebrated Lexington was a loser in a dramatic race, and at a
later time burned in the Sound with great loss of life.

Wall Street bigwigs were calling him Commodore instead of
Captain, and while not inviting him to their homes, were careful to
nod to him as he passed on the street, tall and straight and well
groomed from shoes to shiny silk hat. He had his steamboats, and
his interest in an iron works, in shipyards, and in the Boston & Stonington Railroad.

And now at fifty he built his luxurious steam yacht North Star,

a floating wonder, her satinwood salon furnished in rosewood uphol-
stered with green plush velvet, medallions of Webster, Franklin, Clay
and Washington on the ceiling of the dining room; and he cruised
Europe with his family, a doctor and a chaplain. He returned and
fired a salute of honor to his aged mother in the little farm on Staten
Island, and forthwith went into the transatlantic trade.

Again profit was not the single motive; he was looking into the
future, and what he saw impelled him to put the North Star on the
New York-Southampton-Havre run, and then build other fine ships,
the Ocean Queen, the Ariel and the million dollar Vanderbilt, later
presented to the Government during the Civil War. For this magnanimous gesture Congress gave him a gold medal, which was in
sharp contrast to the verbal lacing Congress gave him on other occasions for unorthodox business practices and commercial intimidation.

But in the 1849 Gold Rush his interest was centered on the
Western Ocean. He had viewed with surprise the huge traffic flowing across the Isthmus of Panama, a bonanza enjoyed exclusively by
the new Pacific Mail Company. He was convinced that superior
service could be provided across Nicaragua, using the country's lake
and waterways. So down to Nicaragua he went and secured a charter
for the Accessory Transit Company to operate a "transit" route across
the country, connecting with two steamship lines.

As one terminal he selected San Juan del Norte (later Greytown),
and on the Pacific side, San Juan del Sur, with a steamship line touching each point. Then when the stage was all set he was startled by
advice from his engineers that it would be utterly impossible to take
the Director up the San Juan River to the lake.

In anger and disgust he hastened back to Nicaragua, took the
wheel of the Director, tied down her safety valve, and as she groaned
and grunted over one obstruction after another to the terror of the
party, he snaked her up the river to safety. Corneel never much
believed in obstructions.

Like everything he touched, the Transit became another gold
mine of profit. Two thousand passengers a month were carried in
boats as far as Virgin Bay on the lake. Then they were transferred to
blue and white carriages drawn by double spans of mules that jingled
across new hard roads the remaining twelve miles to the Pacific. It
was not only a superb feat of business and engineering. It was an
economic attainment, for again it broke another monopoly; it short-
ened the trip to San Francisco by five hundred miles, and it cut
deeply into passenger fares.

But the Nicaragua plot and counter-plot were just taking form. More than one American adventurer was weaving internal political webs. Some strong characters played heavy roles. There was, for instance, thirty-year-old William Walker, lawyer, doctor, journalist, who had run previous filbustering escapades and who with a group of fighting men joined the Liberalists and in a few months made himself master of Nicaragua under the protection of dummy President Rivas.

Washington recognized his de facto government. His brilliant stroke brought enormous popularity; pro-slavery groups regarded him as an apostle of expansion who might annex Nicaragua as a Southern territory.

Absorbed now in the Atlantic trade — he was later to race the Collins Lines off the Atlantic — Vanderbilt had resigned the Transit presidency to Charles Morgan only to learn later of a double-cross that sent his anger above the boiling point. There are gaps in the record, but the facts seem to be that Morgan conspired with others in the company to lend gold to Walker and to give free passage to "emigrants", all fighting men, Nicaragua bound. The payoff surprised even Walker. It was simple: Since the Transit Company had not fulfilled all its charter obligations, Walker was asked to declare it void and to grant the privileges to Morgan and his co-conspirator, Cornelius Garrison. In thus trading a charter for recruits, Crusader Walker blundered badly, for Vanderbilt promptly ousted Morgan and resumed the presidency and leadership in the battle.

But he was, after all, without a charter and so withdrew his ships. Hence there was no service at all to Nicaragua until Morgan got his boats going six weeks later. And when they started moving they carried many "strangers," men who later proved to be Vanderbilt agents, who held secret meetings with President Rivas; and in due course a new uprising came about in which four Central American republics ganged up on Mr. Walker. In 1856 they drove him into the city of Rivas, where ammunition from Commodore George Law and recruits from Morgan were of no avail.

Old Corneel's rage heightened with the months. Finally he sent resourceful Sylvanus H. Spencer and slick W. R. C. Webster of Central America to talk with President Mora of Costa Rica. Mora listened long and gave the nod. Soon a band of Costa Ricans slipped down the San Carlos River to its junction with the San Juan. They seized San Juan del Norte on the one hand and the lake steamers on the other. Walker was isolated from further American aid. Under a flag of truce an American war vessel took him to Panama in May of 1857.

Again Corneel had the Transit and realized he didn't want it after all. So he went at once to his enemies in the Pacific Mail Company, sold them the North Star for $400,000, and then said: "I'll lose a hunk of money if I let the Transit lie idle. And you'd make a lot. I've taken better than a million a year out of her."

Well, what would he suggest? We must of course remember times are hard, "and our recent affairs have been costly."

"Forty thousand dollars a month," snapped the Commodore. They gasped, argued, pleaded poverty, and then consented to this reprisal tax, which he later raised to $56,000 a month; and Pacific still later told Congress amid grunts of disapproval, that for four years they had thus been compelled to pay Corneel the major part of their earnings; "the terror of his name kept off competition."

Most melodramatic of all his struggles, the Nicaragua affair remains a classic in steamship competition.

Sentimentalists wondered what heights of empire might have been attained by blond little William Walker, the man of luminous eyes and strong will, under more favorable conditions. All they knew was that he never gave up his dream of power, and several years later stared cooly into the rifles of a file of Honduran soldiers. Then he crumbled in a heap to the ground.

Old Corneel was seeing a new vision, even while Wall Street whispered that this giant of energy and imagination, with his noble head, white whiskers, pink cheeks and fiery eyes, had had his day.

A stupid Congress had been taxing steamships outrageously, as if determined to run American craft off the Atlantic. Then along came the Civil War to add new havoc.

"Sophy," said the Commodore to his wife one night, "I'm selling all my ships."

"My lands," she cried, "you're restless as a colt with a burr in his tail. What you goin' to do now?"

"Got to do something wuth while. Think I'll try railroads, they're the coming thing."

She protested: "We got piles of money, Corneel, and you're coming on seventy, and ailing."

He rose and took his pile of papers to the library, growling: "That woman never had any sense for business." He seemed to love Sophia in a cold, methodical way, even if he did on one occasion have her committed to a private asylum when she was "goin' through her change," an incident which for once brought the full wrath of old Phebe Hand down on his head: "Get that girl home right now," she stormed, "or you ain't no son of mine. The pore soul borned you twelve children." He promptly obeyed.

Yes, he argued, as he visualized another new era, the iron road was the coming thing, tied tight to the country's future: "It will help develop commerce and civilization, and ought to be encouraged."

And so the fighting Commodore launched his second astonishing career, an incredible, "wuth while" career that in twelve years helped make history.

In his selfish, cold-blooded way he was honest, at least to the point of never betraying a trust, even if he did take his part in the political bribery of the age. And most of all he detested business bungling and disorder, such as existed in the tangled network of little railroads, criss-crossing, cutting throats, and plunging themselves into bankruptcy.

Iron roads, he insisted with honest logic, should run from one basic point to another; by consolidations they should operate as a unit in a given territory and thus afford the public real service. And, of course, the owners a profit.

Once he fixed this pattern in mind, he set about testing the soundness of his conclusions, a somewhat frightening task for a man of such years.

First he must buy up two small roads — the Hudson River and the Harlem lines, later gain control of the New York Central, merge them into one system, and then tackle Erie Railroad, which was battling New York Central. There was sound public justification for such course. Central itself ended at Albany and in warm weather must serve New York over Daniel Drew's steamboats and in winter over the two small railroads.

Wall Street was puzzled if not downright amused when the old steamboat genius started fiddling with the stocks of cheap railroads. The wiser ones stood aside, for they knew him as an eternal Bull on the properties of America ". . . . always buy for investment, never sell short" . . . confident, resourceful, a builder who played for big stakes in the future, and played for keeps.

This philosophy of his was apparent in the Civil War, which like all wars was economic as well as military. He was a staunch friend to the Federal government, a force for victory, and has been called one of Lincoln's biggest assets. For when the Daniel Drew

gang of Bears were pounding values down with every rumor of
Northern reverses, Vanderbilt was pouring millions into the constructive side of the market. He and other men of Wall Street helped
keep the wheels of commerce turning to provide money and supplies.

When he started buying Harlem railroad in the autumn of 1862,
the stock was $9 a share. By the next April he had gained control
of the road and the stock was quoted at $50. Harlem's terminal was
situated in Fourth Avenue. The Common Council of the City granted
him permission to construct a street railway from this terminal down
Broadway to the Battery.

But wait; such rapid success was too much for the Bears. They
put their heads together with Daniel Drew and Tom Tweed; a rumor
quickly flew about that this franchise would be revoked. All of them,
including the City Fathers, sold Harlem short while the Commodore
went right on buying every share offered. Then, indeed, the alder-
men did annul the franchise, and Harlem stock toppled, and everyone
knew that the indomitable Commodore had been booted out of the
iron road business. Of this they were quite sure until they began
trying to cover their "short" sales; it was discovered then that the
Commodore owned all the 110,000 shares of the road, along with
thousands of imaginary shares sold short by the now frantic Bears.
In permitting them to settle with him at $179 a share, Corneel spread
ruin among the Drew crowd and the city politicians and, incidentally,
added a few million to his assets.

"They don't seem to learn that ye ought not sell anything ye
hain't got," said the Commodore.

And they didn't learn. More lessons were in store. Quietly he
had picked up the controlling stock of Hudson and was in Albany in
the winter of 1863 with a bill to consolidate his two roads. There
was no objection until the Bears whispered to the legislators, and the
legislators decided to sell the stock short and then defeat the bill.

Stock again poured onto the market and promptly went into the
Vanderbilt till — 27,000 more shares than existed. The crusty old
Bull was getting annoyed, and when he had them trapped once more
he shouted to his associates: "Put her up to $1,000 a share."

"My God, Commodore," exclaimed the aristocratic Leonard
Jerome, "if we do that we'll break every house in the Street." He
listened to reason and settled at $285 a share, making another thump-
ing fortune.

With each new rail property the Commodore put in excellent

management, proper equipment, and the lines were soon earning and paying high dividends.

"Runnin' railroads is jest like runnin' steamboats. Needs a little commonsense."

And now he was hell-bent for the big prize, the New York Central, then a ramshackle line stretching from Albany, on the West Bank of the Hudson, up to Buffalo. His vision of empire involved a combination of Central with the two smaller roads and a continuous trunkline reaching from tidewater to the Great Lakes.

But here Corneel, the man more feared in old age than any other American capitalist, met up with a hearty, combative crew, a group that ganged with Drew; they put their freight and passengers over the latter's river boats and whenever possible left the Hudson River Railroad to "stew in its own juice." Meantime Corneel kept gobbling up Central stock and biding his time.

The big chance came during a fierce blizzard in January of 1867 when the river boats were frozen fast. Central officials blithely ordered their through traffic to be diverted to the Hudson road again.

To their astonishment they suddenly discovered that Hudson trains were being halted a mile east of Albany on the opposite side of the river. Amid excited protests passengers were forced to drag their baggage across the river to the Central's station in Albany. Livestock and freight from the West began piling up; it was diverted to the Erie, and Central stock plunged thirty points, and Vanderbilt bought every share offered.

Burning with indignation, the legislature subpoenaed him, and the Committee counsel shouted:

"Why didn't you run your trains to the river, Commodore?"

"I wasn't thar," he snapped. "I was home playing whist. And besides this here old law ye gentlemen passed years ago forbids my Hudson to cross the river."

The flabbergasted Committee took the book from Vanderbilt's hand and read the old forgotten law, once passed at the behest of Central to cripple the Hudson road. The case collapsed. Vanderbilt had them in a pocket.

On the following December 11, a single ballot elected thirteen new directors, with Corneel as president and his able son William as vice president, to represent the $18,000,000 of Central stock owned by Vanderbilt. He ordered old cars burned, old engines junked, new rails and ties laid; he put over the three-road consolidation, lifted the capitalization of the new Central $42,000,000, and earnings began to boom.

There followed the adventure with Erie which highlighted the checkered career of slippery Daniel Drew and once and for all took that prize from his grasp.

In his few remaining years, without fraud or scandal, but with stupendous financial daring, the old Commodore acquired still other roads, the Michigan Central, the Canada Southern, and the Lake Shore, broken down properties quickly transformed into highly valuable dividend producers. He did more, commented one New York paper, to restore confidence in railroad management than any other man, even if he did accumulate at least $25,000,000 from the New York Central alone.

To his credit is the fact that he ripped up old iron rails and relaid them with steel; he tore down trembling wooden bridges and spanned the gaps with steel; he improved the rolling stock and built sturdy stations. He put value behind the shareholder's certificate. He helped America expand.

His last seven years were not years of dotage. They were as fruitful as any which preceded them. It was a period of consolidation in which, with the assistance of son William, ablest of the Vanderbilts next to Corneel, and to whom he left his vast fortune, he reorganized and developed his far-flung properties. His faith in Billy, slow to develop, was justified, even if the son was best remembered by a misquotation by a wholly irresponsible reporter: "The public be damned."

Again and again he urged upon William the necessity of preserving the Vanderbilt dynasty. The name must not be forgotten. As one minor step in this direction the Commodore built the St. John's Park terminal, the first adequate terminal within New York city limits, and put up an immense bas-relief of Industry, a monumental horror dominated by a gigantic, fearsome bronze statue of himself in a great fur coat, the only statue of him in the city — all to the embarrassment of the several dozen children and grandchildren.

Sophia had always smiled at talk of posterity. And after watching the ferry boy she had married so long ago rise to the heights of railroad magnate, richest man of his time, she died in 1868. Corneel had been playing whist at Saratoga, where the elite no longer sneered at his grammar and crude manners, but spoke gently of "the delightful old Commodore."

At news of her illness he had raced home, his private locomotive boiling, and lent the entire strength of his iron will to keep her alive. And when medical science failed, there was an elegant funeral, with Horace Greeley and other notables proudly bearing the casket.

The old warrior was lonely after Sophia died. His wrists were no longer strong enough for his high-stepping trotters. Moreover he had been too busy to make companions of his children, and as they grew older they resented the autocratic hand that had ruled them in youth. Billy was different, but even he was slow and analytical, not swift and instinctive.

Corneel was tired of reading and re-reading "Pilgrim's Progress," the one book that seems to have caught the fancy of this great natural economist, a man who probably never heard of Adam Smith. Most of all he craved companionship; and along came a tall, handsome gentlewoman of the Southern aristocracy, whose name was Frank A. Crawford and who had a great grandfather named Samuel Hand, a brother of Corneel's own mother. They eloped to Canada and were married in the summer of 1869.

Without curbing his restless spirit, Frankie Crawford contrived to tame his ruthless intolerance; she weened him from the spooks of spiritualism and soon had him praying for Phebe Hand and son George, who had died in the Civil War, instead of trying to talk to them. She never got him inside a church, but she did get ministers inside the house.

Slowly, skillfully, she tended the crochety old man who was dreaded in his periodic rages by doctors and others; she gentled him into paths of humility; she even tempered his animosity toward charity . . . "them that get charity is lazy . . ." and he found himself giving $50,000 to a church and $1,000,000 to build and endow Vanderbilt University in the suffering South.

She may have lacked the pungent personality of old Phebe Hand, and the self-effacing devotion of Sophia, but she takes her place in the small gallery of women who influenced his character, for when he was dying at the age of eighty-two he murmured:

"I'll never give up trust in Jesus."

He asked for a hymn, and Frankie Crawford lifted her voice, and others at the bedside joined in "Nearer my God, to Thee."

8: Andrew Carnegie : Steel and Books

His astonishing life story surpasses the rags-to-riches fiction tales of Horatio Alger.

Bobbin boy . . . telegrapher . . . railroader . . . bridge builder . . . steel maker . . . titan of industry. And philanthropist on the grand scale, setting a pattern for others.

"He who dies rich, dies disgraced," insisted Andrew Carnegie. His colossal fortune once approached the half billion dollar level. And before he died at 83 he had given away some $350,000,000 for public libraries, church organs, art and music halls, and foundations. In the end he left his family only $25,000,000.

"The rich," he would say to a cheering public, "are merely custodians of wealth to be passed on for public purposes."

At such indiscreet ballyhoo from a "rich socialist" his fellow industrialists would growl their anger. And when this same flaming individualist, the man who would never conform, was lashing his lieutenants to swell output and cut prices, Wall Street was branding him "the little Scotch pirate," who slipped over rebates and blithely broke pool agreements.

Deep down in the Steel King there was undoubtedly a solid core of sincerity and tenderness, a genuine love of humanity which, as described by Elihu Root, began with "passionate devotion to his parents."

"For his was a deeply affectionate nature. When he became rich he went back through his entire life — a multitude of friends — to find who was in need; and he made pension lists of those poor and unfortunate, sick and disabled, and set up trusts for their support . . ."

Cheerful, smiling Andrew Carnegie, with his Scottish burr, his easy flow of polished words, and his amusing and revealing tales, had a singular talent for making friends, friends who loudly sang his praises. Many hitched to his wagon and became millionaires.

But the affable Andrew, with all his phrase-making and his genius for understanding men, sometimes severed priceless friendships, as in the historic split with Henry Clay Frick, whose magic touch as a steel master had swelled the Carnegie fortune by tens of millions. And in Carnegie's late years, when he sent an emissary to seek a reconciliation, Frick boomed: "Tell Carnegie I will see him in hell where we're both going."

But Carnegie had no fear of the hereafter; he died on August 11, 1919, in the serene and justifiable belief that he had made a significant contribution to industry, to his country and to mankind, even though his most noble dream, a dream of world peace, was far from reality.

His life had rather well followed the pattern he had fixed, even though he miscalculated the immensity of the wealth he was to accumulate. For when he had attained an income of only $50,000 a year he wrote a note to himself which came to light half a century later, saying: "Beyond this . . . make no effort to increase fortune, but spend the surplus each year for benevolent purposes."

So thought the Steel King at thirty-three.

Hunger, hardship and deprivation breed big virtues. Carnegie had know them all.

He was born in decent poverty at Dunfermline, Scotland on November 25, 1835, in the attic bedroom of a small stone cottage with red tile roof and dormer windows, one of hundreds of identical dwellings, the first child of William Carnegie and Margaret Morrison. The young couple were too poor to engage a midwife, so Margaret had asked a girlhood friend to fill the role. Margaret always figured things out; like her leather-merchant father, she was a person of unusual intellectual force.

William Carnegie was a weaver. When business was good the four looms in the little house sang their merry tunes into the night; when business was bad he stood on street corners and denounced the crown and the industrial revolution. The Carnegies were radicals.

But for all William's talk the steam loom won out, and it broke his spirit and he cried to his wife, "there is no work."

"Then let's go where there is work," said Margaret. She auctioned the looms and the household goods and made a small loan, and they reached New York in seven weeks on a sailing ship, then by river, lake and canal to Pittsburgh. Andy was thirteen, his brother

Tom six. It didn't much matter that his school days were over; he could read and cipher, knew a bit of algebra and Latin, and was a fair penman. His surprising precocity included a fantastic memory. Always a gluttonous reader, even then he could quote long passages from the classics, a capacity that helped make him one of the greatest dinner table salesmen in commercial history.

Aglow with hope in a land of promise, the Carnegies settled down at their new address: Barefoot Square, Slabtown, Allegheny. Andy's short, sturdy legs were carrying him everywhere, even to the cotton mill where, to his delight, he was hired as bobbin boy at a dollar and a quarter a week. His mother took in washing and stitched boot bindings for a shoemaker next door, a man named Phipps, whose son Henry cemented a friendship with Andy that later carried them to power and fortune. Even Andy's father found work, but he never found courage, and he died seven years later, before Andy could fulfill his promise: "My parents will ride together in their own carriage."

From bobbin boy he moved on to furnace stoker in a dark cellar at a slight raise; then to the gay life of a telegraph messenger in an office of bright boys, several of whom became famous. The foreman, Jacob Larcombe, helped the tow-haired Andy become a telegrapher, and for so doing was handsomely pensioned in his twilight years.

Soon the lad mastered the mystic dots and dashes of the telegraph code and one morning, before arrival of the operator, he violated rules by accepting an important message. The penalty was dismissal. Instead they made him an operator. In months he became one of the few in the country able to accomplish the feat of taking messages by sound instead of reading the characters from a paper sheet.

Such talent attracted wide attention, in time even the attention of Thomas A. Scott, division superintendent of the Pennsylvania Railroad, who promptly engaged him as his private operator at the princely salary of thirty-five dollars a month.

Busy little Andy, just turned seventeen, his ruddy Scotch cheeks glowing with health, had cut his wisdom teeth and sharpened his wits in four years of rough and tumble contact with men. He sensed with accuracy that he was now in on the ground floor with a great pioneering railroad. It was, as he excitedly told his mother that night, a matchless opportunity.

Nor did he miss a chance. In the temporary absence of Scott a serious accident tied up the road. Again violating rigid rules, Andy rushed out a dozen telegrams, stopping trains, shifting others, and moving in wrecking crews that opened the blockade. He signed all messages "Thomas A. Scott." For this new act of "lawlessness" he was made Scott's private secretary.

Said Scott of his protege: "The little devil is a magician. He laughs at difficulty."

Scott put the first investment chance in his way — ten shares of Adams Express — saying to the boy: "Go out and borrow the money." His mother mortgaged the little house, the stock soared and, as Carnegie chuckled years later, "it paid dividends every few minutes."

Off to Altoona Scott took his nimble young secretary, away from Slabtown forever, and there mother Margaret was installed in a nice house with a servant — to her the top rung of affluence.

Discovery that money could earn profits whetted the appetite of the inexhaustible Andrew. His job brought him into contact with investment opportunities, and he quickly mastered the art of borrowing for investment. In a few years he owned stock in a varied group of enterprises: Woodruff Sleeping Car Company, forerunner to Pullman, three oil companies, the Pittsburgh Elevator, two railroads and a bank — all on his meager salary.

And at twenty-four, when Scott became vice president, Andy was made Superintendent of the Division, and settled his family among the lovely estates of a Pittsburgh suburb where he took his place with the folks of fashion. Again, when Scott was made assistant Secretary of War in charge of transportation he sent for his "Scotch urchin" to serve as chief of the telegraph department. In eight months a tangled communication mess was transformed into smooth efficiency; but the task broke the health of this short, tough, closely-knit, hickory knot of a man. He took his mother back to Scotland for a visit and there lay in bed for six weeks. He was, as he said later, one of the first casualties of the Civil War.

Lucky Andrew Carnegie.

He had those qualities that breed success — ambition, tireless energy, a superb digestion, the ability to snatch a quick, refreshing nap in periods of pressure, and a burning desire for knowledge that made self-education a delight.

But important, too, is the fact that he was born at just the right time.

The raw materials out of which his steel empire was fashioned — the so-called Bessemer steel process of freeing iron from its impurities, the Connellsville coke, the Minnesota iron ore deposits, and the era of railroad building — were not brought together until he was thirty-five years old. The first solid tariff wall was erected in 1861, and three years later came the first boom in iron and steel.

Carnegie clearly saw the pattern of the future. His earlier interest in an iron works, he realized, was peanuts compared with the golden field now opening up.

He had organized the Keystone Bridge Company with financial help from top officers of the Pennsylvania Railroad and its dividends of twenty-five percent from the start had paid for his own stock in four years. It was not the first company to build iron bridges to replace the shaky wooden structures, but it became the nation's most prosperous.

Convinced that the prestige of his railroad position was no longer needed, he had resigned after twelve profitable years of service to launch his steel career in earnest. To buttress his fortune we find him flitting in and out of Wall Street and the London financial district, floating big bond issues for railroads and other industries and pocketing enormous commissions.

For his venture in steel making he picked young, strong, daring men — "my geniuses," he called them — and as he had little interest in the manufacturing end, he gave full reign to his eager lieutenants, showered them with bonuses, stock rights and partnerships and created a group of Pittsburgh millionaires.

These men included William Jones, a rare mechanical genius who simplified one process after another, some of his methods still being in use, and who escaped fabulous wealth only because he insisted on remaining in the plant where steel was made.

Henry Phipps, the boyhood friend who had watched Carnegie's mother stitch boots in his father's shoe shop, was a magician at juggling money and making a dollar do four jobs at once. Said one banker: "He could keep a check in the air for days." Phipps handled the financial end. He worked well with able Tom Carnegie, whose lovable ways made for harmony in plant and office.

Then there was happy, warm-hearted Charles M. Schwab who had turned from stage-coach driving to stake driving for Carnegie and who in time moved on to the company presidency.

It was not until much later that cold, wealthy Henry Frick, the

Coke King, tossed in with the group and completed the best balanced, hardest-hitting team in business annals.

When the West began opening up and new roads pushed their way toward the Pacific there developed an insatiable demand for rails more durable than the yellow streaks of brittle iron then in use. It was really at the insistence of Tom Carnegie and his father-in-law, William Coleman, that Carnegie organized his first company to produce steel in 1873. It was called Carnegie, McCandless & Company. The name of banker McCandless gave needed prestige, for Pittsburgh tycoons regarded Carnegie as a dangerous plunger. The panic later that year almost proved their point, but the resourceful Scotsman pulled through.

Even before the new mill was completed Carnegie was flying about drumming up business in the East. His ceaseless efforts brought sheaves of orders for steel rails, orders that soon had Bill Jones smashing production records month on month.

Then the orders became a golden flood. Scorning all practical business details, Carnegie became a superb super-salesman, a gigantic business booster on a scale that made the bigwigs of industry — mostly inarticulate fellows — stare in bewilderment. He was everywhere, talking, clinching contracts, getting lucrative rebates from railroads, arranging rail pools, adjusting tariffs.

And in seven years the Carnegie coalition, though eleventh to enter the field, was producing one-seventh of all the Bessemer steel turned out in the United States, running mills day and night and piling up mountainous profits.

This should have been enough for any one man. But Carnegie found his interests too scattered and inefficient. He decided to put all his eggs in one basket, and forthwith he drew his iron works, bridge company and steel mills into Carnegie Brothers & Company, Limited, with seven partners, but with a majority stock, for the first time, in his own safe hands.

"Faster! Faster!" he cried to his men, coaxing them with cash presents and bigger cuts in profits. Railroads were shouting for more and more steel.

In one period of eight months profits of the steel plant equalled its original cost. By 1881 the bobbin boy found himself the foremost American in the business of making steel; his capital had increased twelve-fold in six years. And in those six years he had sauntered through Great Britain on pleasure trips, jogged about the world, always with an eye to new business, and had written one of his eight books.

Swift expansion necessitated the gobbling up of coal mines, railroads, small steel mills, ore ships and limestone beds. As this process continued the competition in various fields tended to diminish. In such endeavors both Carnegie and Frick were especially adept.

Carnegie had long kept an eye on Frick, a taciturn young bookkeeper, who had bought some coal land in the Connellsville region, which made the best coke fuel for blast furnaces. At twenty-one this genius had talked old Judge Thomas Mellon out of twenty thousand dollars in loans to build ovens, and on his thirtieth birthday he was a millionaire, controlling four-fifths of the coke output in the Pittsburgh district.

The Steel King needed coke, so he made a deal and hitched Frick and his coke supply to the bandwagon and later brought him into the huge steel operation. One would rake the records of industrial history to find an alliance of two men that proved more effective and profitable. Frick was a patient, plodding, imaginative organizer; Carnegie a brilliant, electric promoter of business.

In temperament the two men were worlds apart, and Frick was one man Carnegie never could dominate. Even so, the combination worked so well that by 1889 Frick had been made commander-in-chief of all the Carnegie forces.

He had taken up leadership at a critical time. Over the years a number of Carnegie's partners had been bought out or had passed away. In 1886, most profitable year up to that time, death had taken able, dependable Tom Carnegie, and within three weeks Carnegie's mother had also died. This, incidentally, released Andrew from a promise not to marry while his mother lived. So at fifty-one, with streaks of grey in his cropped beard, he had married the charming young Louise Whitfield, who was a steadying influence for the remaining thirty-one years of his life. He gave her the New York mansion and bought a castle in Scotland, with bagpipers greeting the new day, to the annoyance of a pageant of world famous guests.

Frick was a positive genius in making new expansions pay for themselves. He doubled profits in his second year of operation. A group of Pittsburgh firms had combined to build the great Homestead steel plant as a competitive challenge to Carnegie. Shaky management and labor wars brought on paralysis, however, and it was scooped up by the Carnegie group and made to pay for itself in two years.

One of Frick's most brilliant achievements was the later acquisition of the Duquesne Steel Company, the last word in efficient steel making. It, too, had been built by a group of iron makers and loomed as a genuine threat. It was bought for a song and paid for itself in the first year. The story of its immense earnings reads like a fairy tale.

America had snatched the steel leadership of the world from England. Even before the first skyscraper arose Carnegie had sensed the trend of modern architecture and had installed machines for fashioning beams and girders and steel pillars. Rushing headlong to the forefront of the parade, his name became synonymous with steel in many lands and his production figures were a source of growing wonder.

In 1892 there was formed the Carnegie Steel Company, Limited, "a single organization," as one historian wrote, "with one mind, one purpose, one interest. The annual earning power of this great institution increased under Frick's direction from $1,941,555 to $40,000,000 in a dozen years."

From the profits of the biggest single year Carnegie received $25,000,000, Frick $2,600,000 and Schwab, who became president at thirty-four, $1,300,000. In those days there was no income tax.

The company had attained undisputed dominance in America's most important industry.

Frick whipped the sprawling empire into a complete industrial unit. The scattered works were tied together by the building of the Union Railway. Various roads had been whining about their "rights" inside the company yards. Frick ended these complaints by setting all the roads "outside the fence." The saving on switching charges paid the interest on the cost of the entire road.

Then the ejected railroads quickly granted rebates of twenty-five cents a ton on ore. Thus the private railroad, like the Homestead and Duquesne steel works, was made to pay for itself in a matter of months.

Over and over again, in one field after another, similar methods were applied to cut intermediate costs in the production of Carnegie steel.

Finally, attention was turned to ore. Harry Oliver, another genius who had been a messenger with Carnegie, had purchased a large tract of ore land on the Mesabi Range. Here Frick engineered another fabulously profitable deal. For half a million dollars he bought for the Carnegie company a five-sixths interest in property that became worth tens of millions of dollars. Other important ore options were also quickly picked up, and on October 9, 1897, Carnegie wrote Frick: "I am happy that we are now secure in our ore supply; it was the only element needed to give us an impregnable position."

Yes, the company's position appeared impregnable. But there were smoldering fires within the organization. It was inevitable that Carnegie and Frick should clash; the remarkable thing was that the split was avoided for thirteen years.

In mind and temperament the two men were incompatible. Carnegie stood for the patriarchal system in industry, for one-man power, for promotion only of those who proved obedient. Frick stood for the corporation system, for rule by the directors.

Like an earthquake the quarrel of the two giants shook the business world in 1899. They began warring in public, openly, bitterly, firing charges and counter-charges, and the public began getting its first fleeting glimpse of the wealth of the steel empire. When things looked dark and hopeless, with prospect of a long court battle, the famous lawyer, James B. Dill, stepped in and effected a settlement, for which his fee was one million dollars.

Under the terms of this settlement the mammoth steel company and the great Frick Coke Company were consolidated into The Carnegie Company, capitalized at $320,000,000. The ousted Frick, then fifty years old, received $31,000,000, half stock and half bonds; Phipps received $35,000,000, and Carnegie $174,000,000, also divided equally in stocks and bonds. The remainder went to sixty junior partners and the heirs of deceased members of the parent firms.

Frick's close friend, Andrew Mellon, cabled his congratulations from London.

Frick and Carnegie never spoke again.

With Frick's steady hand no longer holding the reins, Carnegie had less peace of mind, less time to write articles for thoughtful journals, less time to chart new books, and to dream of his colossal philanthropies. He greatly missed his brother Tom, and he regretted that his own wife had not given him a son as well as a daughter.

For the first time in his life he was genuinely unhappy; and problems of business were growing apace, for at the turn of the century a transition phase was developing. A new group of bold fighting men were invading the field, challenging the Carnegie pre-eminence.

Mergers were coming with breath-taking swiftness. John W. (Bet-a-Million) Gates launched his American Steel & Wire Company; the daring Moore brothers of Chicago, William and James, founders of Diamond Match and National Biscuit, packed into one combination some 265 tin-plate mills; J. Pierpont Morgan set up the $200,000,000 Federal Steel Company and put able lawyer Elbert H. Gary in as president.

As he watched with concern the forward sweep of these new and fearless rivals Carnegie knew there were but two courses open. He must assume more active direction of his empire or he must sell out. His final decision was to sell, but it must be on his own terms. Of that he was determined. A tentative deal to sell to Rockefeller at an earlier time had fallen through; as it proved later the Oil King could have made the purchase at less than one-third of the ultimate sale price.

In all his brilliant career Carnegie's genius never touched such heights as those attained in the campaign to unload his mighty holdings. With the pack at his heels, he had whirled and launched an offensive unmatched in business history.

"Sell out? Preposterous! Why, The Carnegie Company is just entering a period of unprecedented expansion." He raced about like an inspired fanatic, trumpeting a series of new projects which would drive competitors to cover and make him absolute dictator of the steel world. There he was, a multi-millionaire, down from his Scottish hills, running amuck with a force and fury never before displayed.

"I will have but one profit from the ore to the finished product," he stormed.

To fight Rockefeller in transportation, he ordered seven huge ore-carrying ships. To fight the railroads, he set surveyors at work mapping a road from Pittsburgh to the Atlantic. To fight National Tube he ordered men to clear five thousand acres for a huge new tube works. Near Pittsburgh a new rod mill would take care of American Steel & Iron.

And, as a postscript to steel companies, he announced he would spend ten million dollars in plant changes, changes that would cut mill costs below all competition.

Such intrepidity by the hardened warrior with thirty-six years of battles behind him was too much for the trade. It was seized with panic by the swift, sure strokes of the steel master. A babble of voices of protest only added to the confusion and consternation. Finally these voices melted into one single outcry: "At all costs we must buy out Carnegie!" That was the cry for which he had waited.

The crowd ran to Morgan, who had also been waiting for a turn in the tide. Morgan and Schwab began negotiations. And before long the most stupendous sale in history had been buttoned up, lock, stock and barrel, and at a price just under half a billion dollars. The "little Scotch urchin" had become the second richest man in the world. And Morgan, tossing in ore lands Frick had bought from Rockefeller, and numerous other properties, created the United States Steel Corporation, America's first billion dollar industrial colossus.

Wall Street guessed that Carnegie's fortune was around $500,000,000.

There it was, the mountain of wealth, the fruit of an unbelievable business career of a boy from Dunfermline, Scotland.

Happy, perfectly adjusted in his new freedom, bouncing Andrew, still youthful in spirit — he had seventeen years remaining — set about the task of giving away the money; he wanted to be useful to mankind, "just like my friend Gladstone," right up to the end.

He built some three thousand free public libraries in the English speaking world, with his name stamped on each. He founded the Carnegie Institution of Washington, Inc., by special act of Congress, for research and investigation in the interest of broadening the knowledge of man.

He set up technical schools, art galleries, music halls, the Carnegie Foundation for the Advancement of Teaching, pouring out millions to retiring professors and their widows; he established hero funds, relief funds, and in 1911 created the $125,000,000 Carnegie Corporation of New York to support and develop institutions previously established.

Vast sums of Carnegie money have gone for economic research, medical education, public health, legal advancement, scientific research, and efforts toward world peace.

Any criticism heaped on him while his wealth was in the making was soon buried in the spontaneous, unprecedented outpouring of love and public commendation that made him a figure of world popularity, with a prodigious flow of fan mail.

When he died at his magnificent estate, Shadow Brook, in the Berkshire hills he was remembered as a great humanitarian in the prayers of all churches, including the 7,689 to which he had given organs.

The nation conceded that he was an industrialist who had helped his country move forward.

Said the admiring Elihu Root: "He belonged to that great race of nation builders who have made the development of America the wonder of the world."

9: John D. Rockefeller : Oil and Gifts

A little blue bowl stood on a chest in the living room of the modest Rockefeller cottage. One day when John was a serious-faced lad of seven he deposited in the bowl the first two shillings he had ever earned. Then gradually, with regularity, he added to this nest egg by hoeing potatoes and catching wild turkeys. And at the age of ten he was able to lend a neighboring farmer fifty dollars, fixing the interest rate at seven percent. Before he had stopped accumulating money Wall Street had estimated his wealth at a billion dollars, making him the richest man in the world.

Unlike many of the early aristocratic fortunes built by land barons, stock jobbers and rail promoters, the immense Rockefeller wealth was perhaps the most honestly acquired; it was amassed by creating a gigantic producing business and in developing a new system in industry that contributed enormously to the nation's industrial progress.

Yet for forty years loud-mouthed politicans castigated him, linking his name with greed, hypocricy and corruption. They were cheered on by thousands of incompetent little business men who held fast to out-moded, inefficient methods and who, because of their numbers, had the support of the politician, the press and the pulpit. They dragged him before Congressional Committees where he was grilled, accused, held up to scorn, and his every act dissected for public edification.

But as often happens, the politicians over-played their hands. Long years before he died at ninety-seven the public had reappraised his great work in retrospect. It had looked with growing admiration upon the disbursement of his fortune for the welfare of man. In a poll it voted him one of the greatest of Americans, and it made each successive birthday the occasion of glowing testimonials. The cloud of artificial hatred had faded, and over the fruits of his career there descended a lasting patina of goodness.

72

It was back in 1722 that the first Rockefeller, Johann Peter, drifted over from Germany. From this prolific, long-lived strain came John's father, William Avery Rockefeller, a big, swaggering, somewhat mysterious fellow with an irrepressible streak of wildness, who in 1837 married Eliza Davison, to the marked distress of her prosperous farmer father.

He set his wife up in a little house on a patch of ground near the village of Richford, New York, and it was here that John Davison Rockefeller was born on July 8, 1839.

William Rockefeller, in pursuit of his trade, which was the sale of a medicine supposed to cure all ills from hangnails to cancer, ranged far and wide, and usually returned home after long absences with a pocket full of money. He would pay up the pressing bills and again disappear. As her family increased, Eliza's economic worries grew apace. But like the mothers of Vanderbilt and Carnegie, she was a woman of extraordinary courage and resourcefulness. She was also deeply religious.

Somehow she clothed and sent the children to a one-room school house until they could "write and figure," and John even had two years at an academy where the tuition was three dollars a term, and an extra twenty-five cents for fuel. His record as a student there was not distinguished.

William Rockefeller finally took his wife and five children to Cleveland, Ohio, after two previous stops in New York state — Moravia and Owego — for the purpose of broadening his own field of operation. A pitch man likes new territory and new faces.

John was tall for his fourteen years; he was strong and quiet, had a long, narrow face and bright eyes, and a fondness for sitting alone, deep in concentration on his problems. This power of concentration and analysis increased measurably in high school and in Folsom's Business College where he studied bookkeeping. In two years, armed with his graduation certificate, the piety and discipline of his mother, and the crude but practical instruction of his father, he found a post as assistant bookkeeper in a produce firm at a total salary of fifty dollars for the first three months.

When this prophet of the modern business era launched his career, other boys — Carnegie, Edison, Armour, Hill, Harriman and Morgan — some younger, some older, were also standing in the wings of the giant stage upon which was to be enacted the colorful and fantastic drama of American business.

He was old for his years, this dignified lad with the high brow and thoughtful, measured words. If he lacked the sparkle and brilliance of the nimble Carnegie, he exuded a fine sturdiness of character that inspired confidence. He practiced self-denial that excluded all but church work, and in his notebook, with its precise rows of figures, he entered his religious contributions, which totaled nearly ten percent of his meager income.

He was definitely marked for success, a success in which he always insisted God played a leading role. At eighteen he and Maurice Clark launched their own produce commission firm and it prospered from the start. Young John could borrow money everywhere; he was the bankers' dream of a desirable risk.

He had heard much talk of petroleum even before Edwin Drake set in motion one of our largest industries by striking oil at Titusville, Pa., in 1859. But mostly oil had proved a pest. It seeped out of rocks, glazed the surfaces of brooks and spoiled the water for cattle. Floods sometimes washed it up on grazing lands and ruined the soil.

Samuel M. Kier and others skimmed oil from Northwestern Pennsylvania streams, or soaked it up with woolen blankets, bottled it, wrapped it in gaudy circulars, and made it the Great American Medicine of the 1840's.

But new uses were multiplying; its cost was far below "coal oil," made from shale. As early as 1854 Prof. Benjamin Silliman of Yale, analyzing a specimen submitted by George H. Bissell, replied:

"You have a raw material from which by simple and not expensive process you may manufacture very valuable products."

So when the cry "OIL! OIL!" swept the countryside after Drake's discovery, the mad drive on Titusville was like a gold rush. Farms were bought up, oil rights leased, and wildcatting broke loose on a grand scale.

Back in Cleveland a group of solid business men listened to conflicting, tangled reports of what was transpiring. They wanted the facts, and so decided to send a trustworthy investigator to Titusville. They looked about carefully and then agreed unanimously upon "young Mr. Rockefeller" who was still just under voting age.

By rail to Meadville and then by horseback overland through the forest trails, the future Oil King finally arrived at the theater of action, and the scene of mounting confusion was painful to his orderly mind. The tiny villages of Franklin, Oil City, Tidioute and Titusville were like big fantastic ant hills; along the creeks and the Allegheny River tall derricks dotted the landscape and thin smokestacks poured black grime over the once green farms. Wagoners cursed and lashed their horses with blacksnakes, and drunken men already were reeling from the doors of shacks that provided whiskey and gaming tables. Out of the compounded confusion the meticulous Rockefeller drew sound basic conclusions. There were, he decided, three aspects of this business: production, refining, and transportation. The cost of coal oil from shale made a shift to petroleum absolutely certain. Yet petroleum production was harried with such uncertainties as wild competition, fires, drastic price swings, and the unknown extent of supplies.

Returning to Cleveland he made his report: "Stay out of the oil business. But watch it. Once a steady supply is assured, consider the refining end, but leave production to those willing to gamble."

Even the prophetic Rockefeller, as he looked in amazement and fascination out over the wild hubbub of the Titusville field never dreamed of the power this new industry was to wield over the affairs of man: nor that petroleum would some day be termed the lifeblood of industry and modern warfare; that our country would come to produce fifty-four percent of the world's total output.

It would be sheer romancing to say he visualized millions of motorcars racing over the landscape, fleets of oil-powered airplanes circling the globe; ocean liners, submarines, railroad engines, farm machinery, plants, mills and factories, all powered by petroleum and, year by year, driving America to greater and greater productive heights.

What he saw chiefly was the possibility of profitably refining oil, and he held fast to that thought for a few years while the oil supply increased. And then, in 1862, with partner Clark, he established the firm of Clark and Andrews. Samuel Andrews, a desperately poor young mechanical genius, was one of the first to see that kerosene would supplant coal oil as an illuminant, and he was struggling bravely with a tiny refinery. The partners put in a few thousand dollars each.

New wells were coming in so fast that the plague of over-production was wrecking the infant industry; the first oil gusher at Rouseville caught fire and killed ten people. Crude oil fell to ten cents a barrel. The age of invention, of iron and steel, of sleeping cars and reapers, and of endless mechanical improvements was dawning, and men were already talking of "Combination" to correct the waste, disorder and incompetence which had been blindly worshipped as free competition.

Rockefeller sold his commission business to Clark and bought the latter's oil interest for $75,000. Now he was completely engulfed in the ceaseless labor of developing a fast-growing business which needed more and more capital. To solve this problem he drew into the firm Henry M. Flagler, a dashing fellow of imagination and exceptional virility, son of a minister, who was married to the niece of rich Stephen V. Harkness. Harkness provided new capital.

Soon Rockefeller was buying direct from the wells, doing his own hauling, turning out kerosene at the lowest coast of Cleveland refineries, and bidding for the western and southern trade. By 1867 brother William had been set up in New York for the export trade under the firm name of William Rockefeller and Company. Rockefeller had paused for a day in 1864 to marry Laura Spelman, a school teacher, but spent part of the day at business, where he treated workmen to a dinner. "But keep them working," he told the foreman.

Railroad rebates were common in those days. When the firm became the largest of the thirty violently-competing Cleveland refineries, Flagler and Rockefeller prevailed upon the Lake Shore and Michigan Central to grant special rebates. Soon thereafter the Rockefeller refineries were rated as the largest in the world; they owned their own wooden tank cars and warehouses. And in 1870 they decided to incorporate under the name of the Standard Oil Company of Ohio, bringing all their properties together. Rockefeller received 2,667 shares; Flagler, Andrews and William Rockefeller 1,333 each; Harkness 1,334; O. B. Jennings 1,000, and the firm of Rockefeller, Flagler and Andrews 1,000 shares.

This was a forward step, but not enough. The old-time reckless, wasteful, throat-cutting competition was, in Rockefeller's own words, "idiotic, senseless destruction," to which most historians now agree; it made for sensational ups and downs, recurrent periods of opulence and distress, and violent and ruinous price swings.

While he abhorred a chaotic system which accepted failure and bankruptcy as commonplace, and while he constantly talked "cooperation and conservation," he did not originate the scheme known as the South Improvement Company, an association of leading refineries. In fact he entered half reluctantly under pressure from other important figures in the industry, fully expecting the plan to fail. Nonetheless he and his associates took nine hundred of the two thousand shares. South Improvement became a classic in business history, and the basis for political agitation for anti-trust laws.

Briefly, South Improvement's contract with the railroads provided for rebates to those companies in South Improvement, varying as to point of shipment, and ranging from 25 to 50 percent, all neatly noted in the contract schedule. Secret rebates, it must be remembered, were a part of the business ethics of the day. So Rockefeller and associates were neither better nor worse than their contemporaries; through their genius and drive they simply carried the device of railroad freight rate discrimination to a perfection never before attained.

Besides the special rebates on all oil shipped by member refiners, South Improvement was given "drawbacks" on all oil transported by competitors. Obviously, under such circumstances competitors were at a hopeless disadvantage.

Standard Oil Company doubled its capital stock to $2,000,000 on January 1, 1872, the day before the organization of the South Improvement Company was completed.

With the stage thus set, Rockefeller and Flagler approached the owners of the twenty-six independent Cleveland refineries. What was actually said is confused in the prejudiced reports of the day. But on one point all seem to agree. Rockefeller offered to buy out the wobbly independents at valuations to be fixed by two appraisers, one selected by the independents and one by the Standard Oil Company. In each case the seller had the option of either receiving full payment in cash or the equivalent of stock in the Standard Oil Company.

In later years Rockefeller reiterated that those who elected to take Standard stock, which he urged, ultimately received many times their own extravagant valuations of their plants. For those who preferred to take cash he felt "only regret at their lack of faith." They were the ones, he said, who led the outcry against him in subsequent years as they watched Standard Oil stock skyrocket to undreamed of heights. Said Rockefeller:

"Every refiner in the country was invited to become a member of the Standard Oil Company, and to participate in every benefit which this most aggressive competitor could secure. That had never happened before in the old system of competitive struggle. The weakest competitors were contemplating stepping down and out; it was only a question of days or weeks. . . . Their anxiety was very great." Standard Oil, he said, told them: "We will take your burdens, we will utilize your ability, we will give you representation; we will unite together and build a substantial structure on the basis of cooperation."

Within three months public clamor, which in the producing fields

mounted to threats of an uprising, had forced the railroads to repudiate their agreement with South Improvement. But in the meantime,
and to the ultimate good of the industry's development, twenty-one
of Cleveland's twenty-six refineries had accepted the Rockefeller
offer, most of them happy to leave a business in which they had
lost faith.

By this stroke Rockefeller became master of about one-third of
the refining business of the entire country.

"You can't keep such men down," William H. Vanderbilt said,
and all agreed that Rockefeller was a captain of industry blessed with
singular genius. He never was a promoter, which Carnegie described
as a man "who threw cats and dogs together and called them elephants." He never carried on stock market campaigns, never sold
stock to the public. He was interested in but one stock — Standard
Oil — and wanted to keep as much of it as he could for himself.

Hardly had South Improvement Company drawn its last breath
before there was formed a loosely-knit group known as the Central
Association of Refiners, with Rockefeller as president. Theoretically,
the component refiners ceased to be competitive with one another.
Actually, however, this shaky alliance exercised but weak control
over a widely-fluctuating, hysterical, and often disastrous business.

In his continued search for a method of stabilizing the tumultu-
ous industry Rockefeller consulted with his brilliant legal aide, Samuel
C. T. Dodd. This same Dodd, as an eloquent young Pennsylvania
lawyer, had earlier helped destroy South Improvement Company.
His blazing attack on that group became a classic indictment of the
immorality of railroad rebates. Such talent should not be lost and
so Dodd was drawn into the Rockefeller fold.

In the course of time it became apparent that Rockefeller and
Dodd had found the answer to their problem; the company's expansion was stranger than fiction, and by the eighties it was controlling
more than ninety percent of the refining business of the entire country.

Mystery surrounded the mechanism by which Standard rapidly
rose to such heights until the facts were brought out by a committee
of the New York State Senate. Then it was learned that thirty-nine
corporations had turned over their affairs to an organization having
no legal existence. It was independent of all authority. Under the
agreement this group of men had united to do things no incorporated
company could do.

"It was," wrote the committee, "the original trust."

Attorney Dodd, who had lost his voice but retained his legal brilliance through a long career with Standard, skirted the obstructions of law by the curious adaptation of the familiar "trust" — the customary legal means through which courts impose a solemn obligation on the custodians of property belonging to widows and others.

The formula was simplicity itself. Under Dodd's guidance, the stockholders of the various Standard and associated companies delivered their stock to nine trustees, including Rockefeller and his brother William. The trustees had permanent and irrevocable power of attorney. With such complete control, they managed all the companies as a unit; they distributed the profits pro rata to the stockholders. When Dodd picked up the word "trust" it was synonymous with "confidence" and "truth." After 1882, the dictionaries set forth a new definition: "A combination for the purpose of controlling or monopolizing a trade." It was a forerunner to the age of trust-busting.

Good or bad, Dodd carved a place for himself in the legal history of the nation. Guided by the genius of his chief, he pioneered the oil trust to monopoly; he pointed a road that other industries began to follow.

By 1888 the word "trust" lighted up the bristling platforms of political parties. The following year President Harrison asked Congress to give "earnest attention" to combinations of capital commonly known as Trusts, and in a matter of months John Sherman of Ohio had introduced a measure that became known as the Sherman Anti-Trust Act. Hardly a voice in Congress was lifted in opposition.

In the subsequent battle, not Washington but certain states led the way. An Ohio decision, and one in New York, put an end to the Trust device fashioned by Dodd, and in 1892 the Standard Oil Trust and similar combinations built on the Dodd model were dissolved.

But even such clear-cut legal action failed to slacken the surprisingly powerful drive of Mr. Rockefeller's far-flung empire. He always pushed forward. In his many battles he could wait with infinite patience, calm and unruffled, and at the propitious moment strike with the swiftness of Napoleon, and move forward, always forward.

Under a favorable state law the Company interests were reorganized as the Standard Oil Company of New Jersey, a holding company, and not until 1911 did the United States Supreme Court declare this new combination a violation of the Sherman Act and order its dissolution. The Company then distributed to its stockholders the securities held in the thirty-seven separate companies. Thereafter each company operated as a separate and independent unit under its own board of directors and not under the Standard of New Jersey board. Rockefeller's health had forced him to relinquish his heavy daily duties years before, and after this court decision, although he had remained president of Standard of New Jersey, he turned complete management over to his associates and to his able son John D. Rockefeller, Jr.

As the greatest money maker the world had known, it is estimated that when he first began lightening his duties in 1896 his fortune did not exceed $200,000,000. But he had set a firm pattern and had chosen brilliant, daring, lieutenants who, under his ever watchful eye, continued piling up the fortune to bewildering heights.

These men, who held forth at the magic address of 26 Broadway, included John D. Archbold, as executive head, Henry H. Rogers, James Stillman and William Rockefeller. The latter three, under the leadership of Rogers, became known in Wall Street as the Standard Oil gang, after they had embarked on an era of feverish and audacious adventure which Thomas W. Lawson immortalized in iniquity as "Frenzied Finance." Their sensational speculations had no connection whatever with Standard Oil and were not participated in by John D. Rockefeller. They did, however, build further fires of public criticism for the Company.

Rogers was credited by Wall Street with invention of a system by which control would be obtained of sound companies in various fields. The companies would be reorganized and additional stock issued — some times to the extent of 100 percent. Then the stock would be sold to the public, with huge profits to the promoters. Rogers' originality might be questioned, however, for an Englishman, Ernest Terral Hooley, had been using the same mechanism in Great Britain some years earlier. In any case, the Rogers group amassed great fortunes. And, curiously, many buyers of the watered-down stocks became rich, in spite of what seemed bad judgment in their initial purchases.

Rockefeller, like a good shoemaker, stuck to his last. When the giant United States Steel Corporation was formed his name appeared among the directors. It was his first directorship outside of his many oil companies.

By reason of his intense concentration, in spite of all handicaps, and in the face of continuous and unrelenting harassments, his great company spread out like a flood, and a day came when its stations and its wagons covered the earth. In a hundred languages the words

"Standard Oil" were household words; through the forests of the Upper Ganges elephants carried his oil on their backs; it rode in tin containers on the shoulders of men high in the mountains of Tibet. Long before Rockefeller died his company had 162 import stations in the foreign service. There were 5,000 foreign distribution stations, thousands of foreign tank wagons, and thirty manufacturing plants abroad.

Rockefeller knew but one way to do things and that was on a Gargantuan scale. And it was on such scale that he determined to distribute his immense wealth to the betterment of mankind.

Never in his long life did Rockefeller make vulgar display of wealth. He held in high disdain certain rich contemporaries whose ostentation blossomed in race horses, yachts, castles and pompous social pageantry. He looked upon such pretension as magnificent foppery.

To him, over and beyond his business, the church, the Baptist church, from early childhood provided all the elements of a full and inspiring spiritual life. He knew his Bible like a bishop and had a massive, unshakable faith, a faith at once astonishing in a man whose hill of gold had grown so high.

He knew where this gold eventually was going, and when it saturated his oil industry and spilled over, he put it where it would grow still further, in iron ore lands and coal lands and railroads. And on occasions when the nation's economy was shaky and his flashy contemporaries were in money trouble, he would put his gold to work in Wall Street banks and in wobbly industries and help to restore order. The mighty Morgan, himself a churchman, but who hated Rockefeller's piety, on such occasions saluted his courage and his sterling character.

Even Theodore Roosevelt, who as trust-buster in the age of muckraking instituted suits against thirty-nine big combinations during his second term as President, had an occasional kind word for the Oil King, for Roosevelt was capable of friendly, side-long glances at the men of wealth when votes were involved.

But one bitter critic, the voluble, capricious William Jennings Bryan, was unyielding to the end, pouring forth his stream of vituperation, studded with righteous phrases, against Rockefeller and all his kind, for which word magic he collected handsome fees. Yet Bryan and Rockefeller were alike in one characteristic. By prayer and contemplation each was able to convince himself that his purpose was God's purpose.

"I have," said Rockefeller, "the most radical, old-fashioned ideas about the duty of every man to contribute to the betterment of his race. I believe that the power to make money is a gift from God — just as are the instincts for art, music, literature, the doctor's talent . . . to be developed and used to the best of our ability for the good of mankind. Having been endowed with the gift I possess, I believe it my duty . . . to use the money for the good of my fellow man."

Such was the philosophy developed long before the river of gold started flowing from his store house. As early as 1890 he began to organize a system of philanthropic giving as a means of securing the most efficient disposal of his treasure. Just as he pioneered the oil business, he systematically distributed the largest group of gifts ever made for the promotion of man's well-being.

He had given away $150,000,000 even before the Rockefeller Foundation was created under a New York state charter on May 14, 1913. His initial gift to the Foundation was $100,000,000. Rockefeller Institute for Medical Research had been founded in 1901 to aid investigations in the sciences of medicine, surgery and allied subjects, and its record is one of glowing achievements. The Laura Spelman Rockefeller Foundation, later merged with the Rockefeller Foundation, was created in memory of his wife to advance human welfare in all parts of the world.

Rockefeller Foundation, under the able direction of John D. Rockefeller, Jr., has held firm to its original magnificent concept in distributing wealth for the "acquisition of knowledge, the prevention and relief of suffering, and the promotion of any and all the elements of human progress." By the time the Foundation was fifteen years old Rockefeller had poured out more than half a billion dollars of his fortune. The work goes on, and today the Foundation stands as a monument to the noble philosophy of a man whose name will grow in history.

One by one his former enemies revised their views of Rockefeller's character. Wrote the editor of one paper which had inflamed hatred against him for years: "A better and broader dissemination of great wealth could scarcely be imagined."

In the long fight to regain his health Rockefeller had applied a strict routine of diet and exercise. He took up golf and played the game with methodical determination, his day of glory being on October 30, 1912 when he made a 39 on nine holes. As an old man he was somewhat of a spectacle on the golf course, pedaling his bike from one shot to another, his old colored caddy following along with clubs, umbrella, raincoat and rubbers. Each stroke was written down with strict care, and Rockefeller was deeply shocked on one occasion when he observed a minister companion surreptitiously kick his own ball out of the rough in an effort to win the match.

In his twilight years Rockefeller believed that his greatest gift to society was his planning against the untamed and destructive forces of an unregulated economy and the building of an industry that provided labor at good wages to an enormous number of workers. While his impact on American business progress was unprecedented, he indulged in no such immodest boasts.

He is best remembered by the public as a very old man, kindly, tall, emaciated, his face wrinkled like the hide of a walrus, a black skull cap concealing a hairless head. On moderately warm days he could be seen walking about the neighborhood of his somewhat plain winter home in Florida wearing a fore-and-aft peak tweed cap with ear flaps, and a scarf wound tightly around his neck. As he passed along the street little boys would smile and address him politely and he would smile back, knowingly, and pass out shiny new dimes.

To the end of his life, whenever the matter of his wealth came into discussion, he would say:

"God gave me the money."

10: J. Pierpont Morgan : Banks and Mergers

Wave on wave of consternation had been sweeping the land as the panic of 1907 tightened its iron grip on the economy. In cities and towns from coast to coast bankers and businessmen, shaken with fear and red-eyed from loss of sleep, were busily casting up accounts and praying for a miracle that might let them ride out the spreading storm.

For a fortnight the New York home of Pierpont Morgan had served as the hub of national finance, and there once again on this memorable night of November 2 the presidents of trust companies and banks, responding to a call of their imperious leader, had assembled in his marble library with its Renaissance masterpieces and magnificent tapestries.

Now in his seventy-first year, the grizzled old warrior with the piercing eyes was utterly spent and secretly wondered if he could fight through another exhausting night without physical collapse. He knew that the fate of the country rested upon his shoulders, for he was, by all odds, the outstanding figure in American banking history, the unchallenged ruler of Wall Street. Through sheer force of personality and financial generalship he had come to exert an unparalleled influence on American enterprise. In his long life he had never shown weakness, and now with the climax of the panic at hand his leadership must be inspiring, commanding, even arrogant and threatening if need be.

He had hurried home from Europe, where there had been minor panics, and had found the stock market weak and uncertain; new issues had glutted a tired market, commodity prices were sinking, and in October the storm clouds had broken and the great panic was on.

Over-extended speculators had begun to unload and, as the process continued, banks and trust companies were subjected to runs and soon the weaker ones were plucking at the covers. By one light-

84

ning move after another the mighty Morgan had temporarily held the dikes. He had marshaled the wealth of his own and other banking companies, putting it where it would do the most good in stemming the flow of panic. He was indeed serving as a one-man federal reserve bank.

And now with money fearfully tight he must make a final momentous effort. In his mind he had decided that his own firm would guarantee twenty-five million dollars for the purchase by the Steel Corporation of Tennessee Coal & Iron and thus save the collapse of Moore & Schley and avoid a chain reaction of brokerage failures. But he would make this deal contingent upon the trust companies raising among themselves another twenty-five million dollars to meet the still pressing obligations of their own group.

As the long night wore on Morgan sat quietly in a room apart, receiving reports of progress from the depressed and hopeless bankers who yearned only for an end of the nightmare. Benjamin Strong made his report on the dreary affairs of the Trust Company of America and, believing his job was done, went to the front door to depart. He found it locked. The key was safely in Morgan's pocket; men left such meetings only when an agreement had been reached.

The men heading the trust companies were beside themselves. How, they reasoned with each other, would they dare make further staggering commitments without even consulting their directors. With dollars as scarce as hen's teeth, where would they raise more funds?

Shortly before sun-up Morgan stepped into the library and surveyed the group of disheveled, despairing men. After a pause he nodded to his attorney. His plan was read aloud. Then he held out a gold pen.

"Sign here, gentlemen," he said.

There was an awkward pause, an ominous silence.

"Sign here," he repeated in a rumbling voice. One by one they stepped forward as in a daze and penned their signatures.

The tide of panic thus had been turned. The old man unlocked the front door. Now he could sleep.

It was not the first time the master of mergers had revealed his terrific force of personality in times of crisis. Men had come to hold him in awe and to give weight to whatever he said, for he was sparing of words and never used them lightly.

Only when his extraordinary career had come to a close was

the full measure of his reticence realized: There had been no stuffy after dinner speeches to be preserved in fancy covers, no pontifical interviews with the press, no signed magazine articles, ghost-fashioned to order. The regal Morgan regarded such public volubility as plain claptrap. And because he was unwilling to be written about, most of the printed material on his life, with a few notable exceptions, either drips with flattery or condemns with brazen disregard of facts. On some points most historians agree. Morgan stood by his word, and he provided unprecedented leadership in a period of national growth when such leadership was sorely needed.

He lived like a prince in New York or London or aboard his sumptuous yacht, and he behaved like a gentleman, even when being pummeled by investigating committees. He never went out of character.

By background, environment, and nature Morgan was a gentleman. Unlike Vanderbilt, Carnegie, Rockefeller, and others who climbed to riches and power from most humble beginnings, Morgan was born to rising wealth in the home of his grandfather, Joseph Morgan, at Hartford, Connecticut, on April 17, 1837.

Grandfather Morgan had put his profits from hotel-keeping into a fire insurance company and built a small fortune. Junius Spencer Morgan, Pierpont's father, had moved from Hartford to Boston and thence to London where he became a partner in the American banking house of George Peabody. In the course of time Junius headed the house and it became J. S. Morgan & Co.

Pierpont was educated in splendid institutions of learning in America and abroad, traveled widely, and when at the age of twenty he launched his career with a firm of New York merchant bankers he had superior basic preparation. His judgment and power of analysis soon became apparent in substantial and daring transactions in which the risks had been measured to a nicety that assured success. Much has been made of the fact that he was the son of a rich man, that he became his father's American representative in an age when London was the great money center of the world, and when American industry depended largely upon British capital and overseas investors for the life-blood of expansion. A study of the record is convincing that nothing short of the continued bad health suffered in his youth could have blocked his rise to greatness, regardless of family status.

He managed his early business affairs with singular genius, and at thirty-four combined his firm (he had gone in for himself) with that of the Philadelphia Drexels, who also had strong overseas connections.   The firm of Drexel, Morgan & Co. soon became a leading distributor of United States government bonds which, like rail and other industrial shares, had to look to the foreign field for investors.

As his career unfolded there was less and less talk of his advantages of birth, for he was attaining that prestige and leadership which one day would make him the most powerful man in America.   Men turned to him first because his mind could take in the raw material of industrial confusion, distill it, and bring forth a finished plan, logical, efficient, smooth and polished as an ivory sphere.

They came to him with tasks too big for other men.   For example, William H. Vanderbilt long had been embarrassed by the size of his immense holdings of New York Central railroad stock.   He wished to dispose of a considerable volume secretly and privately and thus avoid rumors of money distress on the part of himself or the road.   He turned instinctively to Morgan who, without a ripple in the markets, quietly distributed the large holding to London investors. And, incidentally, to represent his London investors Morgan was given a place on the road's board of directors.

This new post was especially helpful in contacts with London stockholders, for Morgan was better informed and better prepared to answer their perplexed and sometimes angry questions.   They wanted to know why our currency was so unsound; why buccaneers like Gould and Fisk were permitted to bludgeon and plunder properties in which honest English money was invested.   They particularly wanted to know why so many American railroads were mismanaged with scandalous disdain for public rights.

Morgan had pondered this matter of disgraceful mismanagement of vital properties.   With his inborn passion for order he developed a downright hatred for the scrambled confusion and financial legerdemain of the unregulated railroads of the eighteen-seventies.

He had had a close-up view of the savage and unbridled competition and the bitter fight for speculative control when, at thirty-two, he had aided President Ramsey of the newly completed Albany & Susquehanna in a battle with the wily Jay Gould.   The covetous Gould had sought control with bags of money, with injunctions from crooked judges, and finally with armed thugs who battled to hold a key tunnel against oncoming locomotives.

Ramsey's subsequent victory in the courts had no influence on the over-all corruption, turmoil, jumble and waste in the rail industry, a condition repugnant to Morgan's systematic mind.   As his influence rose higher over the years he dreamed of an orderly, peaceful, prosperous industry. The problem he faced was not unlike that faced by John D. Rockefeller when the oil industry was at its chaotic worst.

Specifically, Morgan wanted an end of throat-cutting in the matter of freight and passenger rates. He wanted roads to stop bankrupting each other by building parallel lines in regions amply served by one line. He wanted to kick stock-jobbing, market-rigging plunderers out of management control.

His first masterly achievement as railroad peacemaker took place aboard his yacht, the Corsair. The Pennsylvania Railroad and the New York Central were smearing on war paint and preparing to invade each other's territory. Morgan reasoned long and hard with the presidents of the two roads; and the Corsair docked only after complete and hearty understanding had been reached.

Such striking attainment added to his stature and made possible a later compact among the anthracite coal roads to restrict production to needs and to discontinue destructive price wars.

His resolve to enforce discipline and solid business practices strengthened with each success. At length he was cloaked with the power to assemble the heads of all leading railroads in his Madison Avenue home where he proposed a general and lasting peace.

But the result proved only a temporary expedient; it did not correct the deep-seated sins of gluttonous management. It took the panic of 1893, the subsequent major depression, and the bankruptcy of many of the leading railroads to really bring matters to a head.

His previous successful record in reorganizing various roads, reducing their fixed debt and enforcing clean management — pleasing to courts and stockholders alike — now brought to Morgan the gigantic task of reorganizing the broken down major railroad companies. The fees were prodigious. But so was the value of service performed.

Morgan had certain inflexible principles he imposed upon the roads, such as banishing spendthrift managers. He meant to put an end to the gay carnival of speculation. He wanted no more of the do-or-die competition for which the public was paying in dollars and inconvenience. These essentials he laid on the line.

Accordingly, in this reorganization period of the mid-nineties Morgan placed the reborn roads in the charge of boards of directors on which he and his partners or his business associates served and on which they wielded strong influence. In some instances he set up voting trusts authorized to choose a board of directors annually.

Morgan and his associates made no claim to knowledge of practical railroad operation. Their responsibility, as he viewed it, was to protect the companies financially, insist upon prudent management, provide decent service for the public, and build profits for the stockholders. The results constituted an achievement rarely equaled in the long stream of commercial history.

And before the turn of the century more than half of the major transportation systems of the country were under the guiding hand of banker John Pierpont Morgan. He was referred to as the emperor of American railroads.

In the very midst of the rail reorganization program Morgan was called upon to help save the credit of the United States. President Grover Cleveland was desperately worried. Post-panic conditions had shaken confidence at home and abroad, and the Treasury's reserve of gold had dwindled until in early 1895 it had almost reached the vanishing point. Congressional expedients had shored up the supply only from one crisis to the next. The flow of gold to Europe must be stopped.

Morgan had now headed the London house of J. S. Morgan & Co. for five years. His father had been killed on the Riviera when the horses drawing his carriage had bolted. His American firm carried his name only, J. P. Morgan & Co., although it continued operating as a unit with Drexel & Co. of Philadelphia.

Such was the great force of his character that now when he accepted the gold shortage task men looked for success. He was an imposing figure, six feet tall, big chested, with a large-featured face, grey eyes, and an ample mustache. Like other Wall Streeters of distinction he wore a silk hat, frock coat, winged collar, and a broad Ascot tie. He was handsome in spite of a strange skin disorder that gave him a bulbous, glowing nose. Women liked him and flocked about him, but he was first and last devoted to his wife, the former Frances Louise Tracy, whom he had married at the end of the Civil War. He was, even then, a young widower, for in 1861 he had married the lovely Amelia Sturges, who was dying of tuberculosis. He had held her on her feet during the brief ceremony and then hurried her overseas to warmer climates, but in four months his "Mimi" was dead.

When Morgan was drawn into the campaign of stopping the flight of Treasury gold the dangers to the country, as he confidentially cabled his London office, "were so great scarcely anyone dared whis-

per them." The biggest single immediate obstacle to sound government credit was the continued sale of American securities by Euro-
peans who were worried over business bankruptcies here. Such
sales enhanced the flight of Treasury gold.

White House lights burned night after night as the Cabinet
struggled with the problem. There was not time to float another
bond issue. And to do so in January, only three months after the
last one, would simply advertise to the world that the situation was
desperate.

After discussions with an official of the Treasury who had
hurried to New York, Morgan worked out a detailed plan for meeting
the contingency without compelling President Cleveland to fight
things out further with a Congress tinged with the free-silver philosophy of the Populists. What he proposed, briefly, was a private contract by the Government with a syndicate to market fifty million
dollars in bonds, the contract "to be considered a state paper and
confidential and not to be divulged until the issue is completed. . . ."

While negotiations were moving forward hopefully word leaked
out that Morgan and a syndicate of other bankers were coming to the
rescue of the gold reserve. Confidence was restored for the moment,
stock exchange prices moved upward, and for several succeeding
days the outward flow of gold almost ceased.

But there were new breakers ahead. Suddenly Democratic
newspapers launched an attack; they were horrified that any private
deal should be made with a Wall Street banker who, even worse, was
a Republican. Pulitzer's New York World warned Cleveland that he
was turning the Treasury over to the powers of wealth.

In a twinkling the deal was called off; Cabinet members argued
that the crisis had passed, that the outflow of gold had ended.
Morgan was deeply shocked by this turn of events. He knew that
improvement in the markets, based on hope of successful negotiations,
would change to panic and disaster for the Government if the private
sale plan were abandoned at this late hour. With his attorney Francis
L. Stetson and young partner Robert Bacon he started off to Washington, determined to lay all the facts before Cleveland himself.

His reception was as cold as the icy wind that whipped about
the station platform on his arrival. Secretary of War Daniel Lamont
met him with the news that Cleveland would not see him. To avoid
public notice, Morgan then drove off to the home of a friend where
he sat alone most of the night playing solitaire and planning strategy.

Next day, February 5, word came that Cleveland had given in

and decided to see him, and in an upstairs room in the White House the burly, worried President said flatly: "We have decided to make a public issue of bonds."

With deep sincerity, and in sparing words that ranged far and hit hard, Morgan sketched the ominous over-all situation; his tremendous certainty was irresistible. The only possible success, he insisted, lay in quick private action. Then he played his trump card. He called attention to an old law of Civil War days which authorized the Government to buy coin and pay for it in bonds.

Under the terms of this law, he argued, the government could buy gold coin which the syndicate would gather in the United States and Europe and pay for it with the proposed new private bond issue.

"Mr. Morgan," asked Cleveland," "will you guarantee that while we are getting gold in it will not be shipped abroad and thus prevent us reaching our goal?"

Here Morgan made an unprecedented commitment. "Yes, sir," he said. "I will guarantee it during the life of the syndicate. That means until the contract has been concluded and the goal reached."

Said Cleveland years later: "I had a feeling of watchfulness. I had not gone far, however, . . . until I found I was in negotiation with a man of large business comprehension and of remarkable knowledge and prescience . . . of clear-sighted, far-seeing patriotism."

Simultaneously the new bonds were put on sale February 20 in London and New York. That afternoon Morgan's London office cabled: "Subscription enormous. Subscription books closed at noon." And Morgan cabled back: "We have closed our books. . . . Quite overwhelmed by success of transaction. . . . Sincere congratulations."

There it was. The job was done, and by June the Treasury's gold reserve crossed the safety line of one hundred million dollars. Dire calamity had been averted.

But there were screams. The more blatant members of Congress still insisted Morgan and Wall Street were the enemies of man, and stories were circulated that Morgan and his associates had netted sixteen million dollars on the deal. He flatly refused to tell Congress the sum of his profit, and later it developed he had done so only at the request of August Belmont who had helped stem the tide of escaping gold.

Half a century later the able Frederick Lewis Allen decided to run down the facts of this controversial point of profit. He set them forth in his interesting book, "The Great Pierpont Morgan."

Of the American Syndicate's total profit of $1,534,516.72, the
Morgan profit, including interest gain, was $295,652.93, out of which
came the costs of carrying through the transaction . . . "a modest
recompense indeed for saving the credit of the United States."

It is not the nature of builders like Morgan to stand still when
new challenging ventures continue rising on the horizon. Accordingly, from railroads he moved on into other industries and became
the greatest corporate promoter of the age. After the storms of the
mid-nineties had taken their toll of failures a new swelling tide of
confidence gradually developed and on this tide Morgan rode to the
crest of his power.

Many industries, such as the steel business, were in need of reorganization, especially since men now were talking of national markets,
and of efficient production and distribution methods to replace wasteful local marketing methods. New Jersey provided the legal mechanism for combinations. The governor was seeking new ways to
increase state revenues and he turned to lawyer James B. Dill who
cleverly charted the course. A law was enacted which permitted
the creation of holding companies. Under this law a single company
might be formed with perfect legal confidence to buy the stock of
a number of companies and thus, with far-flung facilities, go after
the national market.

It was this law, highly profitable to New Jersey's exchequer, that
set in motion a whole new series of combinations, including the giant
merger in steel, the biggest business promotion of all time.

Judge Elbert Gary had come from Chicago to consult Morgan
on a new combination by John W. (Bet-a-Million) Gates who, with
Gary's help, had merged a number of steel and wire companies and
now was consolidating a still larger number in his eighty-million-
dollar American Steel & Wire Company.

Before the subsequent series of conferences had ended Morgan
had embarked with Gary on a deal to tie together several concerns,
including Illinois Steel Company and certain ore properties, to form
the Federal Steel Company, of which Gary became president.

In the summer of 1900, while the ferocious struggle within the
industry was reaching its climax, with Carnegie cracking out new
expansion plans which made certain that his secret desire to sell his
own properties at a top price would be realized, the stirring thought
swept through the industry: Why not combine the combinations.

Within a year the mighty Morgan had engineered creation of the colossal United States Steel Corporation which embraced under single management some three-fifth of the nation's entire steel business.

When the deal was closed, Morgan congratulated Carnegie, whom he had never particularly liked, on being the richest man in the world. A year later when the two men met on shipboard Carnegie remarked that he feared he had made a mistake in the price he had fixed when he sold out for just under half a billion dollars.

"I should have asked you a hundred million more," said Carnegie.

"You would have got it," said Morgan — a disturbing thought that may have haunted the great Scotsman the rest of his days.

As to the immense merger itself, William Jennings Bryan expressed the view of his admirers, who, incidentally, were dwindling in numbers with improving times: "Whenever Mr. Morgan doesn't like America he can give it back to us."

Crowds of curious people began hanging around the Morgan offices at 23 Wall Street in the hope of catching a fleeting glimpse of the famous man who was now head and front of American banking power. They dogged his footsteps on the Sabbath when he went to worship, which he did with regularity, for he was senior warden of St. George's and one of the leading laymen of the Episcopal Church in America. He was no hypocritical psalm singer, but professed a stout belief in the Bible as written, was deeply impressed by the formalism of his church and devoted much time over the years to its welfare. The story is told that he suffered his most humiliating defeat on an occasion when he sought to cut St. George's vestry from eight to six members; he was getting old and felt a smaller number of rich men, meeting at his home, could expedite the church's financial program. He was challenged and humbled by the great liberal rector, Dr. William I. Rainsford, who forthwith increased the number of vestrymen, and in spite of this daring rebuff he and Morgan remained warm friends.

Morgan's frequent trips to Europe in his late years brought gaping crowds to the piers on both sides of the Atlantic. He would pass through these lines and across the gangplank, straight and stiff, with never a side glance or a wave of his walking stick.

Even on these later trips he was bent on business — the business of art. When he decided to become a collector, the art world at last saw a man of action. He astonished both buyers and sellers in his successful raids upon the private collections of Europe. He never quibbled over price; he simply bought what he wanted. And he wanted many things of beauty — ivories, crystals, jades, miniatures and Bibles; and most of all he wanted paintings by the masters and these he continued to buy and ship back to America in huge cases. Before he was through he had helped fill the magnificent Metropolitan Museum of New York, and as its president he ruled that treasury of art with a strong and steady hand. His collections at their peak had an estimated value of some thirty-five million dollars.

In the selection of art his usual restrained taste was evident. It was evident, too, in his innumerable gifts, whether they involved masterpieces or funds for new college or church buildings. In philanthropy he made his own decisions, swiftly, quietly, without publicity or pomposity. To him spending for mere show was as distasteful as the glitter of lavish social pretension, reflecting a certain lack of character.

And character was the rock to which Morgan clung. A bit of his philosophy on the importance of character impressed a hardbitten Congressional committee shortly before he died.

This committee had set out in 1912, as such committees are often wont to do, to prove its preconceived beliefs, and the process was aided in a measure by the selection of like-thinking witnesses. This so-called Pujo Committee was determined to show the existence of a "money trust" of bankers, led by Morgan. Its final report, after months of satisfactory headlines, did indeed reveal some imposing statistics on the extent of the Morgan influence, buttressed as it was by the influence of bankers George F. Baker and James Stillman. Between them and their partners and members of their boards they held 341 directorships on banks and trust companies, transportation companies, insurance companies, producing, trading, and public utilities companies. Of this total Morgan partners held seventy-two directorships.

To climax the hearings the grizzled and ailing Morgan, then in his seventy-sixth year, was dragged before the Committee for two days of pitiless probing. He had been dismayed by the growing popular distrust of wealth, intensified by a wave of unbridled muckraking; he could not comprehend the significance of the new concept of social justice.

Nervously, relatives and counsel stood by as the old man was helped to the witness stand, fearful that he would collapse under the ordeal. The gawking crowd saw that age and weakness had erased his once frightening mein and that the blazing eyes were now tired and faded. But the will was strong, and he fought back on the basis of his lifelong principles and beliefs; he gave the crowd glimpses of a character that had inspired such confidence among the titans of finance and industry as to carry him to world fame and power.

With all the vigor he could muster he denied over and over again that the Morgan firm actually held controlling power by reason of these many directorships. On banks and industrial corporations his partners were in such a minority position, he claimed, that by no stretch of the fancy could they exercise control. What influence they had was based upon their personal integrity and their talent in providing superior guidance in fiscal matters.

Repeatedly and with emphasis he returned to a single point in his argument. He insisted that the most important thing in business was the ability and character of men who had funds or properties in their custody. He underlined the word character.

"Is not commercial credit based primarily upon money or property?" asked the examiner.

"No, sir," the old man snapped. "The first thing is character."

"Before money or property?"

"Before anything else. Money cannot buy it. . . . A man I do not trust could not get money from me on all the bonds in Christendom."

And the motionless crowd which had anticipated a public confession of guilt was deeply impressed by the tremendous sincerity of his words.

At last they helped Morgan from the stand, and he departed for Europe pondering the strange turn of national psychology and asking himself whether his government would ever again call upon him except to grill him about his past. In four months he was dead. He passed away in Rome on March 31, 1913, and friends insisted death was due to the "strain of inquisition."

The man whose name was synonymous with great wealth surprised the public with the relative smallness of his estate. It had been assumed that he had made money on the scale of Carnegie and Rockefeller and was one of the wealthiest men of all time. Instead, he left but $68,000,000, aside from the art collection, a fortune smaller than that acquired by numerous contemporaries. After gifts and personal bequests the estate went to his son J. Pierpont Morgan who became senior partner of the firm.

Under the drive of a group of talented partners the firm went on to become as powerful on the international scene as it was at home; it served as purchasing agents of the Allies during World War I.

As the years passed great private power was removed from American finance, and World War II ushered in the present age of public billions. Hence the House of Morgan operates in a financial atmosphere strikingly different from that of Morgan the Elder, whose genius as a master of mergers and as a promoter of business efficiency remains unmatched.

11: Bright Summer

Like a relentless sea the mighty bull market of the 'twenties swept onward. New millionaires, hundreds of them, poured their quick wealth back into common stocks. The public, stark mad with speculative fever, tried to emulate the exploits of the rich plungers, tried right up to the hour of the most devastating collapse of all time.

Kings of the markets had become oracles whose whispered hints of a new pool or syndicate, when flashed across the land, were enough to launch new waves of public buying that rolled into the New York Stock Exchange and taxed its physical machinery.

Architects of a prosperity as false and fantastic as John Law's Mississippi Bubble were busy fashioning major manipulations, tidal movements in speculation so enormous as to dwarf into insignificance the operations of earlier times. Such was their hypnotic spell over the public that in four years they could drive a single stock — Radio Corporation of America — from $25 a share to $570 on a split share basis, without the company ever having paid a penny in dividends.

From its inception the bull market had been a one-way affair, with the swelling cavalcade of big and little bulls pushing prices ever upward. A few conservative easterners, astonished at the incredible rise, sold short from time to time and always with painful consequences.

Even the realistic Jesse Livermore, the genius once known as The Boy Plunger, tried to short-sell the big market and lost one of the four huge fortunes which he had acquired in a long and colorful career, a career that featured a parade of yachts, mansions, women, bankruptcies, and a self-inflicted pistol wound from which he died on Nov. 27, 1940.

Strangely enough it was Livermore, the bogey man of the bulls, who on December 29, 1923, had first predicted the shaping of an unprecedented bull market. Shortly thereafter another man, the incomparable William C. Durant, began beating the drums of market prosperity.

Livermore and Durant, bear and bull, had created sensations in the post-war deflation storm of 1920. Livermore had sold short and made a new fortune, while Durant, in a desperate and futile fight to retain control of General Motors Corporation, had tossed his fortune of $90,000,000 into the financial whirlwind. Durant was that kind — always playing for big stakes.

Then in 1924 with a new fortune and a boundless enthusiasm for America's swelling wealth and its new position as money center of the world, Durant gathered about him a group of millionaires and forthwith introduced Wall Street and the nation to an era of cosmic speculation.

In the confusion created by the roaring, churning market there arose conflicting reports as to the identity of the members of the Durant group. It was rather well established, however, that it included Arthur W. Cutten, Chicago's wealthy grain speculator who had turned his genius to stocks; and a number of men whose names loomed large in the motorcar industry, including the fabulous Fisher brothers of Detroit. Reports of the day spoke of the brothers as seven former blacksmiths who were merely seeking to invest some $300,000,000, which included the profits from selling their Fisher Body Corporation to General Motors in 1923.

It is fair to assume that at least a score of very rich men placed direction of their speculative millions in the hands of Durant, the "bull of bulls," and that nothing in the bewildering history of Wall Street ever matched the aggregate wealth and speculative power thus drawn together.

In the single year of 1928, according to published reports, Durant handled 11,000,000 shares of stock having a value of more than a billion dollars. His total was almost as great in each of the two preceding years.

Nor was the operation, strictly speaking, a manipulative pool. Rather it took the form of persistent gigantic buying in specific stocks which, statistically, were behind the market and which gave promise of future broadened earnings. Durant and his associates also kept plugging up weak spots in the market as the bull drive progressed.

Concerted bear attacks were bothersome in the early stages. Then the day arrived when the Durant-Cutten-Fisher group, backed by almost unbelievable power, virtually wiped bear battalions out of existence. And in time public speculation became so immense that Durant could ignore the bears; he even liquidated part of the enormous lines and retreated with large profits before the final catastrophe.

Durant's group were not the only magicians of the big bull market. There were many others, men now dead or retired, men whose names once fired the public fancy only to be forgotten in two decades of new world crises.

For instance, there was smiling Harry Content, broker extraordinary for the Guggenheims, one of the wiliest operators on the Street, an old master of markets who, credible reports had it, was a chief factor in the catapulting of Kennecott Copper, long a Cutten favorite. Across the market he moved like a genial Sphinx, mysterious, confident, and deadly in his speculative thrusts.

For his big deals he frequently used George Breen, one of the powerful floor operators, a genius in oil stocks, a doctor of sick markets, and a trader with exceptional talent for pools.

Wide-eyed visitors in the crowded gallery of the Stock Exchange strained for a glimpse of Breen, and were equally fascinated by the "Silver Fox," Frank E. Bliss, another master of pools whose dollar volume of trades for the giants reached astronomical totals as the simmering market came to a boil.

Still other architects of the mountainous market included Benjamin Block, broker in vast commitments for Livermore and Durant, and red-headed Michael J. Meehan, whose rise to wealth was a constant wonder to The Street. A specialist in radio, he was the daring crusader credited with running up the price of RCA more than five hundred dollars a share. Total trading in that rocket of speculative favorites sometimes reached 300,000 shares a day and dragged the whole market with it — a sensational, wholesale speculation that later drew much attention from Congress.

But Congress awakened, as usual, when the show was over. Most members of Congress apparently knew little and cared little of the operations of such men as Joseph E. Higgins, poolster and plunger who rose from curb stock huckster to multimillionaire, or of Louis W. Zimmerman, biggest West Coast plunger, whose colossal orders influenced prices and flabbergasted the trade.

In the unbroken race toward certain collapse the chattering ticker stamped out other names, sometimes those of industrialists whose business and speculative interests had become interlaced in the hurly-burly pageant of the bulls. Every word, every hint, was weighed and acted upon by millions of men and women.

For instance, when John J. Raskob sailed for Europe on March 24, 1928, he commented that General Motors, then at 187, should be selling at 225, or fifteen times its earnings. Next day the stock leaped up five dollars, and the following market day it hit 200 while half a million shares were bought in the insane scramble for new riches.

And speculators, seizing a new yardstick of value, soon had the public convinced that stocks were worth twenty times their earnings. A revitalized bull drive swung under way.

Bright was the summer of 1929. Happiness spread across the land. Glasses tinkled in a thousand glittering night spots where the paper-profit rich gulped down rivers of bootleg booze. Golf clubs were crowded; the tired executive slipped out three afternoons a week, and his secretary rushed off to the beauty salon.

Gangsters were plugging each other with lead, and riveters were plugging steel girders on which were rising ever-loftier monuments of stone. Hitler was just a little fellow with a mustache, needling into action some plug-uglies in Brown Shirts.

It was America's happiest summer, and summer was turning to autumn. Nowhere did faces shine brighter than in the crowded brokerage offices, where all seats were filled early and where by noontime dense crowds gathered, straining necks for a glimpse of a favorite symbol dancing across the trans-lux screen.

In the crowds were men and women born to riches; and cab drivers, lawyers, house maids, physicians, waiters, clergymen, chorus girls, race-track touts, bank clerks and racketeers. It was an all-out parade, a composite rejoicing in the collateral prosperity touched off by the boom in stocks.

Margin requirements were thin, in light of the high prices, and the little man and the little woman pyramided gains, using profits to expand holdings, and meantime spending the paper wealth, through credit, for radios, cars, furniture, smart clothes and homes for which they could never pay.

All summer the speculative fever had almost been matched by a new "sun-tan" craze and beaches were loaded with gay crowds in daring and colorful swim suits, crowds babbling a new jargon of "brokers loans, stock-splits, rediscount rates and industrial averages." A skit in a musical play depicted two white-coated street cleaners doing a graceful, dainty dance and singing a market ditty: ". . . For money is easier today." Everywhere music of the market filled the air; it was Wall Street's most beautiful lullaby, a lullaby that soothed even the great minds into pleasant apathy and stoic stupidity.

On March 4 Calvin Coolidge had left the White House for his
low-cost duplex apartment in North Hampton and his barren little
office where he was busy punching out magazine pieces. He had left
the gathering storm to Herbert Hoover, a great American who probably received more unfair abuse than any other statesman in history.

The first sharp quake shook the market in early September.
It cracked the dike and a flood of selling orders poured through. But
the prophets were ready, and bellowed: "Here's the spot to buy!"
And the public responded, driving brokers' loans to an all-time peak
of eight and a half billion dollars.

But as the month progressed a curious and disturbing softness
developed. Foreign money was being quietly withdrawn, and this
course was hastened by Englishmen, after the collapse of the Hatry
speculative bubble. Each succeeding week registered fading values,
and in the two-hour market session of Saturday, October 19, a major
storm broke loose. Some blown-up issues collapsed as much as forty
dollars a share. People stayed home on Sunday and studied the
financial pages with furrowed brows, and with good reason, for
margins were thinning and the market was honey-combed with stop-
loss orders — orders to sell when the price had declined to a certain
level.

Prices began reaching those levels the next Monday and before
the six-million-share day was over the bright eyes and shining faces
in brokerage offices had become an unbroken pattern of stark fear.
The fear intensified on Tuesday, and deteriorated into dumb stupe-
faction on Wednesday when the deluge brought such extreme drops
as ninety-six dollars a share in Adams Express and seventy-seven in
Auburn Automobile. The "instantaneous" ticker service fell far
behind.

Then came bitter Thursday, October 24, a headlong, roaring
day of terror, a day that found massed humanity, in speechless
bewilderment, blinking in wonder at collapsing values — wealth
evaporating not by millions, but by billions; men and women, vast
numbers of them from coast to coast, wiped out, made penniless, their
hopes shattered, their idols broken. There they stood at the fag
end of a foolish dream of wealth, a dream so ingeniously dreamed
that it seemed real all the time.

Still other millions of people, raking together diminished assets,
put up new margin and went home to tumble about in their beds
and pray that the brave bankers who had come to the rescue would
still save the day. Later they knew the lucky ones were those

cleaned out early and thus spared the agony of baseless hope. For the climax was still ahead.

It came on Tuesday, October 29, a day of unbelievable turmoil and disaster, a day of riotous huckstering, with grinning ruin standing at the side of millionaire and janitor, poolster and plunger, banker and bandleader — an entire nation liquidating wholesale, scrambling madly to save a few remnants. In the deluge that day the great marketing machinery broke down under the weight of more than sixteen million shares of trading, a record figure that may have run many millions more in the confusion. Hours, sometimes a full day, elapsed between placing a trade and learning the consequence, despite the army of red-eyed clerks that kept office lights blazing all night.

On the tragic day of the greatest stock market catastrophe of all the ages some shares crashed as much as sixty dollars — on top of the long succession of previous losses.

A lamp of hope was lighted when old John D. Rockefeller stirred himself to action and announced that he and his son were buying common stocks; but the light soon faded as, day on dreary day, the slide continued until a bottom finally had been reached on November 13, at which point thirty billion dollars in values had ridden off on the winds of liquidation.

It was the rich who were wounded most deeply, whose economies soon closed jewelry shops, smart gown emporiums, perfume and fur stores; they released maids and chauffeurs and gardeners, abandoned home building projects, sold yachts and limousines. It was, indeed, the rich who were jumping out of windows and taking overdoses of sleeping powders.

Harassed executives were soon cancelling factory expansion plans, cutting off unprofitable departments, tightening lines of operation and laying off non-essential help. Swiftly the ripples of retrenchment widened from industry to industry, from class to class and, week by week, unemployment spread across the land.

Official Washington had swung into action and was given the hearty support of commerce and industry. Everyone — industrialists, bankers, merchants and labor chiefs — poured forth optimistic words: Nothing really was wrong with the country, they insisted; the gamblers had simply taken a beating. . . . Wall Street was groggy but Main Street had its chin up and shoulders back. . . . We merely had to get down to work again. The press radiated cheer and sought to inspire courage. Between gulps of bathtub gin sad-eyed people even began

to sing a catchy little song called "Happy Days Are Here Again."
But as time passed and the depression deepened a more honest little
song was sung with genuine sincerity:

> No more money in the bank
> No cute baby we can spank
> What's to do about it?
> Let's turn out the lights and go to bed.

In 1930 dividend disbursements had been especially heavy, not
because of good business but because the rich had been so heavily
punished financially that such policy seemed imperative. A day
came when a former rich stockbroker looked with envy at the mail
man and said: "God, how nice it must be to have a fixed income,
no debts, and a beaming face."

There were few beaming faces. Yet such was the faith in the
country and so stubborn was the conviction that nothing could long
halt its onward surge that the pool operators reformed their shaky
lines and, with public support, put on a little bull market in 1930.
But, unhappily, it fell apart, collapsed in a heap as the inexorable
economic cycle continued its downward turn, continued until the
all-time low base was reached in July of 1932. Then Radio, the high-
flyer that had touched $570 a share, was selling at $2.50; U. S. Steel
was bringing not $261.75 but $21.25; New York Central was not
quoted at its golden age top of $256 but at $8.75, and shares of that
sterling boom day performer, General Motors, were being offered
at $7.62.

Nor was that all. Wheat at forty-four cents a bushel in Chicago
was the lowest since the days of Queen Elizabeth; cotton went for
five cents a pound, and a few angry Indiana farmers showed their
disdain for the economic cycle by burning corn as firewood.

As the clock of history ticked off the doleful months, living
conditions steadily worsened; the corner apple salesman made his
appearance; kindly cigar clerks would sell a single cigarette for a
penny; rumpled, unshaven men squirmed on park benches, trying to
keep warm under a layer of old newspapers. And before the soup
kitchens the dreary lines lengthened.

Business continued sinking lower, lower, lower. Queues of
job-seekers at factory gates sometimes numbered as many men as
were at work inside.

Back in the gleeful days of August of 1929 there were but
1,000,000 unemployed workers. In 1933 there were 14,700,000 seek-

ing jobs—more than one out of four. And despite brave words of
the politicians, unemployment continued to be a problem until war
removed it nine years later.

In the fierce, withering deflation which closed banks and jammed
the courts with cases in bankruptcy and receivership the nation's
nearly half million corporations operated in 1932 at an aggregate
net deficit of $5,640,000.

Such were the conditions into which a presidential campaign
had been injected.

Adversity sets ideas to boiling. Desperate men grow bitter,
hateful and reckless and demand change—any change, but change.
Everywhere the surly mood had become increasingly apparent.
While President Hoover had gone on struggling under the weight of
an overwhelming Democratic opposition his every weakness was
magnified in a relentless bombardment of releases from the Democratic publicity machine, an almost endless out-pouring of diabolic
propaganda. For direct personal attack in spiteful, stinging phrases
the barrage has rarely been equalled in American politics.

Each succeeding blast lessened confidence in the nation's leader
and helped clear the way for the easy election of Franklin D. Roosevelt, who talked, somewhat vaguely, of many things, including the
ill-defined "forgotten man," but who talked and talked and who was
heard from sea to sea.

The biggest bull market in history cast a black cloud over Wall
Street. It also changed the political destiny of the nation.

12: A Pageant Passes

In the blatant, tawdry age that spanned the period from the
Civil War to the fag end of the century the Wheat Pit almost matched
Wall Street in its unbroken series of dramatic episodes.

The harvest of the Civil War was wild extravagance, loose
morals, greed, trickery, bad banking, and politics styled in bribery.
It was a hard, gay era. Grain speculation became a machine-rat-
tling, law-mocking game. Immense deals were planned and carried
out, and periodic panics convulsed Chicago's La Salle Street.

John Deere's steel plow had broken the rich prairies and McCormick's reaper had broadened the grain fields and had resulted, in
1848, in creation of the great Chicago Board of Trade, first a wagon-
load market and later the hub of world grain commerce.

Resting on the eastern rim of the wheat area, and on the north-
east corner of the corn belt, Chicago became the gateway to a vast
and sprawling garden, and finally the leading rail center, and second
city of the nation.

Futures trading, the instrument of enormous speculative drives
in grain, did not begin until the Civil War was underway. During
the conflict the government sought to erase all doubt as to definite
grain supplies at certain future times. So it contracted with responsible individuals to make specific deliveries on indicated future dates
at agreed prices. The method worked, and grain futures trading
became a permanent phase of the national economy. Through all
the intervening years it has remained a political issue.

Almost from the outset audacious men sought quick wealth and
power in the Wheat Pit. These market masters left a trail of ruin
and despair so shocking that lawmakers and responsible merchants
and brokers were compelled to set up restrictions and prohibitions
in the interest of public welfare.

By the turn of the century most of the buccaneers who had roared across the Pit, bawling out orders that paralyzed trade, had been shorn of their money bags or banished to other fields.

Of all the mad adventurers who snatched at the crown of Wheat King none gained the quick, dazzling notoriety of Crazy Harper.

He was a boisterous man, thick set, with a round mask-like face, round glittering eyes, and a needle-point mustache that dipped downward. "To rest is to rust," he used to bellow. "Let's whoop her up!"

That was in the 'seventies when he was a sewing machine agent. His idol in those days was Timothy Dexter, who a century earlier had sent eight shiploads of bed-warming pans to the West Indies, getting rich on the venture.

"I'll put a sewing machine in every hut, cave and igloo," was Harper's loud boast. He did succeed in making a big stake; he went into pig-iron where he made a million, and then vaulted into Cincinnati's largest bank as an officer.

At that time Wall Street's carnival was in full swing, and La Salle Street was dancing and giggling and creating financial scandals.

Until the bursting of his gigantic speculative bubble, E. L. Harper was known in the grain trade only as the Ghost of the Pit, for he had kept his identity well concealed.

Queer antics began in the Wheat Pit in early 1887. Bankers and Exchange officers were puzzled by the vast accumulation of the grain — thirty million bushels in a few days. As the mystery deepened a clique of wealthy men was suspected, but efforts to trace the buying were futile.

Harper had hoped to corner the market in February, seize the crown of Wheat King, come out of his Ohio obscurity and parade the Street in a blaze of glory. But he had misjudged the farmers, for they swept their bins clean and sent a golden stream of new wheat pouring into Chicago. The price cracked and Harper was forced to sell half of his holdings at a heavy loss.

Then of a sudden his wealth seemed to swell; his numerous brokers re-entered the market and cracked out orders that stunned the Pit.

Day after day the price climbed upward. Shorts were driven to cover, and bankers fretted as numerous brokerage houses began plucking at the covers. It became clear that extreme measures must be taken. So a clique of Bear operators was formed and day after day they flooded wheat on the Harper brokers. Again he was compelled to change tactics. So he sold out his holdings at another thumping loss and reinstated them almost at once in the June option. Each of his various brokers then was instructed to buy a million bushels a day. At length his line reached nearly eighty million bushels. His funds seemed inexhaustible.

Markets have a way of foretelling approaching disaster. A curious period of quiet and dead uncertainty sets in. Such a tense interlude took place in the Harper deal. As days passed a feeling grew that the climax to the drama was near at hand. Fear was etched on every face.

Lights blazed high in offices along the Street during the night of June 13. Each house was casting up its accounts and measuring its financial endurance. At dusk Harper brokers had slipped quietly into the old Richelieu Hotel; in the gray dawn they emerged, gaunt, haggard and silent. Dejection replaced the former swagger and nonchalance.

Brokers, scalpers, speculators and the heads of leading houses began filling the Pit early on the morning of June 14 until it was packed to the point of suffocation. There was no loud talk, only whispers. The deadly, tight stillness that heralds a market explosion had fallen like a velvet curtain.

At 9:30 the great gong boomed out, signaling the start of trading. Bedlam broke loose. Sellers fell upon the Harper brokers like madmen. They were offering wheat, millions of bushels at a crack; they tore at the brokers, ripped their coats and shirts to tatters as prices cascaded. Dazed, gasping for air, the Harper men pawed their way to the rim of the Pit for new instructions. Instantly the order came: "Sell it all quick!"

A terrible yell went up. New panic swept the Pit, the building, the whole Street, and the moans of ruined men were heard in every brokerage house. Wheat crashed nineteen cents a bushel before any semblance of order was restored.

Down went one brokerage house after another — twenty in Chicago alone, including that of C. J. Kershaw, chief Harper broker. The ruin spread to Milwaukee, New York, St. Louis and other cities as the fortunes of thousands of men were wiped out almost relentlessly.

To the nation there was further startling news next day when it became known that instead of a clique of wealthy men, a single individual, E. L. Harper, had been head and front of the deal and that he had looted the Fidelity National Bank of Cincinnati of its last dollar.

The Ghost of the Pit, the man who is recorded in speculative annals as Crazy Harper, remained tight-lipped, staring at his accusers with his round, glittering eyes. Only when placed on trial did he break his sphinx-like silence. Then he stated quite simply: "I stole the funds to gain power." He had drained the bank by having the teller withhold checks and count them as cash.

"Did you ever mention these cash items to other officers?"

"Good God, no."

"Did you ever look at them?"

"No. They were like a long line of ugly corpses. I knew one look would paralyze me."

Crazy Harper wandered aimlessly about the prison yard, doing little chores and dreaming of the happy days as a sewing machine agent. As the years passed his health failed and he was sent back to his home. One day he stood with a friend, staring out of a window with unseeing eyes.

"To rest is to rust," he murmured, and dropped dead.

It was the year following the Harper debacle that Old Hutch made his historic stand. He attained the rare, if doubtful, distinction of being the only man who actually cornered the American wheat market. In the fleeting hour of success he could dictate the price of our daily bread.

Benjamin P. Hutchinson was striking in appearance: very tall, lean, and slightly stooped; he had a determined chin, a nose hooked like the beak of an eagle, and narrow eyes that gave off a friendly twinkle. He was born in Danvers, Mass., in 1829 and early developed a hatred of farm chores and heavy blizzards. At twelve he got a job with a merchant in boots and shoes for twenty dollars a year, but resigned in high dudgeon the second year on learning the boss' nephew was paid thirty dollars a year.

On a crude shed next door a bold sign soon appeared: "Ben Hutchinson — Boots and Shoes."

By the time he was twenty-eight he had made a fortune as a shoe manufacturer. Then the 1857 panic wiped the slate clean. He started west with his wife and ended up in the Wheat Pit.

All his life he was a voracious reader. Few could match his

broad knowledge of economics. He loved literature and was a student of Shakespeare.

During his early days in the markets the lank, bony man with the broad-brimmed black hat was something of an enigma to the other traders, a silent, lone wolf who was gaining fortune and power with no apparent effort. Unlike Daniel Drew and other Wall Street plungers of the Civil War days, he was a man of unimpeachable integrity; he took no part in pools and such-like shenanigans. In the Civil War period of unbridled speculation he piled up a fortune from trades in wheat and gold but only by reason of superior genius in foretelling coming events.

Usually he was a Bull. This he admitted with a twinkle when he shook hands with and congratulated General Sherman and General Grant on the occasions of their respective visits to the Exchange after the close of the war.

He was a Bull on the future of the West, on Chicago, on the expansion of commerce and industry. In the course of years he created his own meat packing company, a Chicago bank, and other solid business enterprises. Then on a tragic night he stood on a roof-top and watched roaring flames leap from street to street and con-sume the city in the great fire of 1871. Once again he was flat broke.

It was a blow from which he never fully recovered. He had no craving for wealth, as such, nor for power in the usual sense. But Old Hutch had one dream that influenced his life; he was determined to be Wheat King.

In the ten years following the Chicago fire his successes multi-plied and by the mid-eighties he was again a financial giant; he also was a man of many curious eccentricities, such as the tearing up of letters without opening them. "If it's important men should tele-graph or come to see me."

Then there was the famous Century Club nearby which Old Hutch underwrote and ran, selecting the members himself. The appointments of the lounge were in good taste — thick rugs, over-stuffed chairs, rich draperies and a few oil paintings. At one side of the room, as a sort of symbol of his rugged individualism, stood a barrel of whisky and six shiny tin cups.

At the end of a strenuous market day the select group would gather about the barrel and talk books and music and listen to Old Hutch recite poetry. Market talk was taboo, even in the tense period of the historic corner in wheat.

This corner was begun early in January, not by large accumulation, but by substantial purchases which Old Hutch would follow up with less substantial sales. Thus his holdings increased without attracting undue attention. Before the strategy was discovered Old Hutch had acquired an immense volume of wheat in a period of a few months.

In consternation over this threatened one-man control of the market, the powerful and widely dreaded "Big Four" — Cudahy, Ream, Nat Jones and Linn — leaped into battle against Hutch. Unable to break the market and bring about his ruin, they were joined by the shrewd Partridge and then by P. D. Armour, a titan of the grain trade in those days. The contest became one of a single man against the field.

Crop conditions, said the government report in May, were growing worse, just as Hutch had anticipated from his own studies, and this situation helped to tighten his hold. By July his mastery of the market was virtually complete. Then one day a rumor struck the Pit like a clap of thunder: "Old Hutch is dead!"

A spasm of selling seized the market. But it was short-lived, for Hutch had himself carried upon the floor by four sturdy clerks and placed comfortably in a chair near the Pit. Prices immediately zoomed upward again. Hutch had simply tumbled down the iron stairs at the Century Club, which gave rise to the cheerful rumor of death.

They built a huge chair, six feet high, and placed it at the rim of the Pit and there on "The Throne" sat the Wheat King for the next six weeks, dictating prices, while the press of this and foreign lands poured forth streams of bitter denunciation.

On September 20, 1888, Old Hutch quietly absorbed the last of the offerings from the country, a remarkable feat in light of the fact that no other speculator had ever been able to withstand the eleventh-hour downpour.

"Tomorrow," he observed laconically, "will be a tolerably busy day."

How high Old Hutch had planned to put the price of wheat, as well as the extent of his tremendous profits, were questions never answered. A strange thing happened the next morning. Old Hutch was requested to appear at the office of his own son, Charles L. Hutchinson, who was president of the Exchange.

Above all else Old Hutch loved his son, who later became one

of Chicago's leading citizens, and who had accepted the presidency
of the Exchange only on the promise that his father would defer to his
wishes in all matters concerning market manipulation.

It became the son's unpleasant duty, therefore, to recall the old
man's promise and to ask him to break his own corner, to shatter a
dream just come true. The decision was painful to both.

"Charlie is a good boy, none better," was the old man's only
comment as he hobbled back to The Throne. Then he stared out
over the broad trading floor of the Exchange and bellowed:

"Come on, you whining, white-livered scallawags, step up to
the captain!"

The line formed and one by one the speculators who had sold
wheat short moved up to The Throne and settled their accounts.
Most of them had faced complete ruin. Old Hutch was lenient with
the small fry, but demanded his pound of flesh from the big speculators. He was particularly severe with the proud and stubborn
Armour, who found the experience "the most humiliating" in his
long career.

When all accounts had been settled and the Wheat King eulo-
gized for his magnanimous release of the world wheat market (which
one impulsive editor termed an act of genuine patriotism) Old Hutch
walked out of the lives of his family and friends for a long period
of time.

He had spent a night alone in the low-slung balcony just over
the Wheat Pit. A narrow beam of yellow light was falling on his
face as a surprised attendant came upon him. The old man awakened
and sat for a long time watching the light pour through the stained
glass windows and turn the trading hall into a glowing mass of
Pompeian red and gold. Then he said:

"I have spent a night with the ghosts of my memories."

He walked slowly down the stairs and disappeared. For six
months a nationwide search failed to disclose his whereabouts. On
his return to the Pit one of the most singular happenings in market
history occurred. With almost utter abandon Old Hutch, who had
become quite religious, gradually poured most of his millions back
into the market.

When the chill of old age was upon him he spent his declining
days in a sanitarium tucked deep in the wooded silence of Wisconsin.
His only recreation was an afternoon ride behind a team of spirited
horses. On March 16, 1899, the only man who ever attained the

crown of Wheat King passed away. In his final delirium he talked of the Pit.

It was an age of revolting vanity, and many eager hands reached out for the coveted, elusive crown of Wheat King after the passing of Old Hutch. Men craved wealth and power as never before. A few hungered for revenge. But one by one the strong contenders went down to destruction. The crown remained where the genius had dropped it.

And then came young Joe Leiter, son of the merchant prince; young Joe with his winning smile, his flashing eye, and his vast amount of good sense. He was big and strong, bold as a hawk, and had an ardent desire to be Wheat King.

He was born in Chicago in 1868, graduated from Harvard, and then traveled widely. It had been the plan of his father, Levi Z. Leiter, to place him in charge of his immense real estate holdings, and, accordingly, he advanced a million dollars as working capital.

But Joe had no taste for the prosaic profession of land agent. He thrived best on color and drama and swift action. The roar of the Pit had stirred him like the blast of a bugle. The call was irresistible, and at twenty-nine he plunged into his great adventure.

It began in the summer of 1897 and became the longest single deal in Wheat Pit history. Leiter had shown exceptional talent in his study of world conditions. This study proved that importing countries had grown two hundred million bushels less than the year before; reserves everywhere were low, and among exporting countries the United States alone held a surplus. To buy this surplus was, in theory at least, to make Europe pay through the nose; and such was the daring aim of the young speculator.

He concentrated his buying in the December option. A vital part of the plan was to deplete the stocks of wheat in Chicago. This would prevent the big shorts from making delivery to Leiter during that month. Thus he could push the prices sky high, and with his millions in profits buy more physical wheat to withhold from Europe.

In November he began shipping wheat out of Chicago, first in carloads, then in trainloads. By mid-December the Pit discovered that the "boy wonder" had apparently cornered the market in December wheat.

Still another startling discovery was made. It was found that on the opposite end of the Leiter deal was old P. D. Armour. His predicament had made him savage and uncompromising, flinty and sinister; he had been humiliated by Old Hutch, and he did not intend to permit a repetition by this upstart. He was, nonetheless, short millions of bushels of wheat which, by his contracts, he was obliged to deliver to Leiter in Chicago during December. But he would neither ask nor give quarter.

Here indeed was drama enough for the colorful young plunger. He would not dare challenge the Armour millions and the Armour market skill; he would, of course, throw up his hands and ask for mercy. So reasoned the grain world, at least, and the reasoning was absolutely wrong.

For dare-devil Joe ran upon the trading floor and fairly shouted in glee: "I have the old fox, I have him! He's hog-tied and must settle at my price."

The crowd blinked in astonishment at such audacity, such rash impudence. No one had ever had the temerity to jeer at Armour.

Scowling and grumbling like a wounded bear, Armour went straight to Leiter.

"Young feller, what's ailing you?"

"Not a thing, sir. You've contracted to deliver a little wheat, I believe. Since you can't deliver you must settle at my price."

"I'll never settle!" Armour bellowed over the roar of the Pit.

"Oh, yes you will," taunted the youngster. And then he laughed, laughed outright in the face of the great Armour. That was a blunder; Joe never should have laughed. But he was young and confident and bold.

Armour spoke just two words: "Laugh, Clown!"

His heavy jaw closed with a click and he strode away.

December was the most difficult month of the year for getting wheat into Chicago. There was wheat to be had in the northwest and in Canada, but at this season the Great Lakes freeze over, navigation closes, and marine insurance lapses on all the big inland seas. To Armour, in his flaming wrath, these obstacles were not insurmountable. At least he could try. So he sent a wire to hundreds of agents in the northwest: "Buy all the wheat you can. Concentrate it immediately at Duluth."

Then he gathered a fleet of lake vessels, a few here, a few there, personally assuming the insurance risk. Next he chartered a fleet of tugs and set them to smashing a narrow lane through the ice of the Duluth harbor. He hired crews of the toughest, hardest seamen to be found and paid them handsome bonuses for their hazardous task.

All night long powerful searchlights played streams of fire across the icy stretches, as shrieking tugs pounded back and forth to the open sea.

Other tugs smashed through the ice of the Fort William harbor.

Soon a long fleet of vessels, laden with wheat, began crawling toward Chicago, each boat conveyed by tugs that cut a narrow passage through the grumbling ice.

Leiter got his wheat — millions of bushels of it. Elevators were soon crowded. And he took delivery in high good spirits and held firm, simply switching his futures deals into May. His bankroll could stand the pressure.

By a fortuitous stroke war broke out between the United States and Spain. On May 10, Leiter had a clear profit of seven million dollars. This profit grew as he continued pushing up the price of wheat to foreign countries, and before the end of the month his gains were reported to have doubled.

Right then Leiter should have liquidated the huge line. But success had added to his natural boldness, and he committed the biggest blunder in Pit history when he decided to carry his mountain of wheat over into June, the month when the new crop starts moving.

Then came the deluge. Bears sold wheat short in million-bushel lots. Argentina and India swept the floors and offered wheat to America. Russia emptied her mills and ate rye. Of a sudden wheat poured into Chicago from all directions, by boats, trains and wagons. No one could stem the golden tide. Leiter fought bravely for a time, but the Frankenstein of his own creation brought his destruction.

On June thirteenth the paralyzing blow fell with dazzling swiftness. The whole deal collapsed, tumbled prostrate across a frantic Pit.

The boy plunger, the "smart-aleck young pirate" who had twisted the arm of powerful P. D. Armour, and who had defied all the conventional rules of speculation, was through, finished, a dejected, wild-eyed wreck.

His father sacrificed some choice real estate and sadly picked up the tab for nine million dollars.

Old man Armour sent his photograph to young Leiter, bearing the scrawled inscription: "With best regards —"

In the period since the turn of the century there have been a number of gigantic grain market deals and a few king-size scandals.

For the most part, however, the market leaders have been men of substance, conscious of the big club held by Congress.

Of the many great speculative fortunes drawn from the Pit only a few were retained by the victors.

James A. Patton, a studious and kindly man of high character, had made his millions at fifty-eight and devoted most of his remaining eighteen years to public welfare. His gifts to colleges and charitable institutions were enormous. While president of the Board of Trustees of Northwestern University he gave that institution $1,500,000.

One day in 1927, long after Patton's retirement, I asked him about the so-called Patton corner of 1908. He smiled.

"That was my greatest service to the country," he said. "It was no corner at all. America had a shortage of wheat. We needed that wheat here at home. I bought it and kept it home."

Then he took from a drawer of his desk the old records of the deal which we checked, day by day, and the evidence was indisputable. For it showed that after Patton had sold his wheat, instead of a price collapse, such as would mark the end of a corner, the price actually continued upward. But Patton's judgment paid off in millions and the deal is still referred to as a corner.

And the 1924 wheat deal by the late Arthur W. Cutten is likewise incorrectly referred to as a corner.

Cutten was one of the most glamorous and successful speculators of Wheat Pit history. He had come out of his native Canada as a boy and taken a six dollar a week job with an Exchange firm. In the next half century he rolled up a fortune of a hundred million dollars.

In the post-war deflation of the early 1920's the collapse of wheat prices ruined farmers across the grain belt and closed hundreds of small banks. Wheat had fallen from three dollars a bushel to little more than a dollar when Cutten began his purchases in the summer of 1924, convinced that world conditions justified higher levels. Within six months he had created a boiling bull market in which the public was plunging to the hilt. Incidentally, the writer rode that market to within two cents of its top before selling. It was a big market; for breadth and volume it has rarely been equalled. The price touched $2.05 3-8 before the sensational collapse. Cutten was reputed to have had a fifteen million dollar profit at the top, but this gain shriveled as prices bumped downward. On his smaller gains of 1924, before closing out his big deal the next year, he paid a federal income tax of $545,000, largest in Chicago that year. After the deal ended, the price of wheat climbed back to $1.75, substantiating Cutten's claim of its inherent value.

While the market was going up farmers were happy and government officials remained silent. When the price collapsed, under liquidation, the same officials were horrified and demanded reforms. Punishment for the Exchange consisted of placing a daily limit on the extent of price swings and the creation of a modernized clearing house system. Both were constructive steps.

Cutten soon turned his talents to stocks and helped create the biggest bull market in history, the one that toppled in 1929. When his fortune was at its peak he fretted as to how the money should be dispensed. Among other things he had considered creating a network of small hospitals for the poor. He yearned to leave some worthy monument. During walks home together in the evening he used to tell me of some of his hopes and dreams. With the stock market collapse and the subsequent panic and depression he was relieved of the problem of distributing a huge estate. When he died in 1935, the slender, quiet, gray haired speculator left only a modest fortune to his widow.

Immediately after the New Deal came into existence it did everything possible to create Bull markets and inspire new confidence. The commodity markets leaped into life and cooperated in a flurry of enthusiasm. As the summer of 1933 deepened, the ticker tapes on stocks, grains, cotton, sugar and a host of other items began fidgeting as if Roosevelt might indeed bring about the golden age promised in his campaign.

One man particularly wanted to help bring back prosperity. He was Dr. Edward A. Crawford, who was reported to have been a practicing dentist down in Georgia, then a cotton speculator in New Orleans. Of late his diminutive figure had been moving shadowlike in and out of Wall Street and La Salle Street. He almost made a fetish of looking shabby in his unpressed clothes; his pockets bulged with money.

As the Roosevelt boom progressed the doctor hit the jackpot not just once but repeatedly until he had a substantial fortune and an immense line of credit on thin margin from brokerage houses long starved for business.

If the dollar were devaluated, Dr. Crawford reasoned, the price of commodities would at least double. Common stocks, many selling below cash on hand, could run up from three to ten times current levels, which indeed some of them did. Cotton was a veritable gold mine; fortunes beckoned in rubber, copper and sugar.

In the course of a few months, according to financial journals which may have indulged in some exaggeration, Dr. Crawford pyramided his holdings in options and in "privileges" to eighteen million bushels of rye, thirteen million bushels of corn, sixteen million bushels of wheat, 330,000 shares of stocks, 180,000 tons of rubber, 35,000 tons of sugar, and a large line of cotton.

Not completely satisfied with the size of his hedge against inflation the doctor then took a look at eggs. He became utterly absorbed in the subject and stopped buying only when he was reported to have acquired a total of three billion eggs (probably an exaggeration).

The public had become as reckless as Dr. Crawford and the stock exchange was recording eight-million-share days.

Of course, the inevitable crash came in mid-July. Overboard went wheat, corn, rye, cotton, sugar, copper, rubber, and eggs, eggs, eggs in a collapse only mildly reminscent of 1929. Greatest uproar came from the farmers, and to the end of his life President Roosevelt never got over his bitterness toward the Chicago Board of Trade for "obstructing the recovery movement," which was really an artificial inflationary movement.

Dr. Crawford faced his creditors. Considering his gigantic line, he had moved out with speed, for he had failed for less than a million and a half dollars. Eggs had proved his greatest burden.

A story was told that he later drifted into a Wall Street lunch counter. A fat, voluble waitress, swabbing the bar with a wet rag, paused before him, saying:

"And what will yours be this morning — a nice omelette?"

"God, no!" groaned the kindly doctor.

The Wheat Pit still roars, but it is a gentle roar, like the muffled notes of a distant organ. The robust days are gone. The end of a colorful pageant has passed and faded. Washington is determined that the lush days of big grain speculation shall not return. It is sometimes foolishly argued in official circles that there should be permitted only enough speculative trading to amply sustain legitimate grain hedging by merchants and exporters and processors. Nor is there any large group of voters to challenge such specious conclusion, despite the immense economic importance of the Chicago Board of Trade.

13: Money and Politics

In his historic drive for election in 1948, President Truman declared in Dexter, Iowa on September 18th: "These Republican gluttons of privilege are cold men. They are cunning men. . . . They want a return of the Wall Street economic dictatorship."

Having faced repudiation by his own party, some of whose candidates shunned him as "political poison," Truman stepped out and won a victory surprising even to himself. It was the most sensational upset in American political history.

How many votes were garnered by what were termed his demagogic allusions to Wall Street is not known. But most newspapers headlined the attacks, as they had headlined similar cheap attacks by New Dealers for nearly twenty years.

Yet in the earlier years of that same period the New Deal had enacted numerous laws, including the Securities and Exchange Act, which had changed the structure of banking, and which had put the new Wall Street into a straight jacket as snug as its most rabid critics could fashion.

Displaying exceptional courage, the largest brokerage firm ran a paid advertisement after the 1948 election challenging the President's comment.

"One campaign tactic did get us a little riled," said this advertisement. "That was when the moth-eaten bogey of a Wall Street tycoon was trotted out. . . . Mr. Truman knows as well as anybody that there isn't any 'Wall Street'. That's just legend. Wall Street is Montgomery Street in San Francisco. Seventeenth Street in Denver. Marietta Street in Atlanta. Federal Street in Boston. Main Street in Waco, Texas. And it's any spot in Independence, Missouri, where thrifty people go to invest their money, to buy and sell securities."

From the 1929 market crash onward Wall Street was pictured as the symbol of everything bad. During the 'thirties such doctrine of

118

hate was splashed in the press and poured over the air waves, and proved singularly helpful in perpetuating the New Deal.

Many economists are convinced that the depression and the excessive unemployment of ten years, up to our entrance into World War II, were intensified by public fear, fed by attacks on Wall Street and Big Business.

Certainly business lived in a strange new climate of sociological change in that decade. Labor unions, expanding under the Wagner Act, were hell-bent for power. Strikes were chronic and wages on the march. Workers embraced the Roosevelt theory that "economic royalists" sought to grind them down to a bare existence. Political and labor attacks on business were not vastly different from Russia's later attacks on "capitalistic America."

A truce in the New Deal's cold war on business came of necessity when World War II began. Freed of the blistering attacks, the industrial machine moved into high gear and began performing production miracles.

Yet in the midst of the greatest business boom in history, in the war and post-war years, a strange thing happened. So deeply had public confidence been wounded by the persistent attacks on big business and speculation that Wall Street and the Stock Exchange passed through a period of hard times. Instead of a roaring bull market, based on large corporate earnings, there was a restrained bull market that toppled in 1946 at a time when the business boom was racing onward to higher levels. Subsequently many Wall Street houses began operating in the red and continued to do so until the pressure of inflation forced a flow of excess funds into common stocks. Government contributed to such inflation through lavish non-defense expenditures and through its lending and monetary policies.

In that period of market doldrums tall-browed economists struggled with the problem of why risk capital, so essential to national progress, had gone into hiding. Such venture capital is the very heart blood of the industrial machine. Population had swollen to 150,000,000 persons; we were attempting to feed part of the old world and supply recovery equipment. Yet corporations, desperate for new risk capital, were forced to borrow from banks and insurance companies and draw on reserves for necessary expansion. Aggregate loans outstanding of government agencies for the post-war period from December, 1945, to March, 1950, increased by 143 percent as against a loan expansion for all commercial banks of 67 percent.

Nimble tabloid thinkers with leftish leanings argued that the financial system, which had helped build the nation, was discredited and doomed; we must move into the beauty and light of a regimented society.

To other thinkers the shock of President Truman's sudden change from the role of a conservative mid-westerner to that of an advocate of leftish laws and a welfare state involving staggering expenditures was too much for those with money to risk in new ventures.

Investment money did indeed pour into savings accounts, government bonds and insurance, but not into venture expansion. A fear complex, a desire for security rather than risk, seemed to permeate all classes, even to the college graduates of 1949. That class of 150,000 sober young Americans was not burning with dreams of great achievement. Most of them, according to a poll by a national magazine, simply wanted a good job for life.

Deep in the hearts of people was a fear of the future, a subconscious fear, built layer on layer, largely of the outpourings of left wing political opportunists.

Such opportunists took advantage of the fact that some of the American people had not quite made up their minds what kind of a government they wanted. They had not chosen resolutely between free enterprise and some form of statism. They would like private ownership, along with some of the touted security features of collectivism, but without the suffocating evils of collectivism.

Plainly, risk capital, that substance which induces expansion and creates jobs, feared a drift into collectivism, a drift, incidentally, which was aided unintentionally by powerful pressure groups.

Each pressure group — labor, veterans, farmers, merchants, social uplifters, flood controllers, and educators — bedevils Congress for special grants that favor a particular class, grants involving huge expenditures, grants that chip away at the foundation of the democratic form of government and point the way to collectivism.

Most congressmen of both major parties are too sensitive, too vote-conscious, to stand firmly against pressure groups of constituents, even in the face of evidence justifying such a stand. Too often they bow to the philosophy that government can take care of all the people better than they can take care of themselves. So the march toward ultimate socialism went on.

Our system calls for a dynamic economy, an economy of growth. Logic dictates the release of the natural forces of human beings, millions of them, across the land. The urge for survival is strong. Given freedom, the American public responds and increases its earning power. We must not stifle enterprise by wanton government waste and devastating taxation. We must sweep aside policies that even tend to drive venture capital into hiding, if the country is to grow and the high living standard is to be maintained.

It would be sheer nonsense to try to whitewash the early mistakes of business or of Wall Street, or to defend conditions incident to the collapse of 1929, a collapse for which politicians, brokers and bankers shared responsibility with a gambling-mad public. Yet it is equally stupid and economically dangerous to continue pounding "Wall Street" for pure political gain.

Wall Street is no longer a money lane ruled by a few lords of privilege; it is made up of millions of Americans who hold stock in corporations — merchants, doctors, lawyers, engineers, teachers, clerks, housewives, laborers, bankers and artists. It has long been the heart of our financial system, founded on a free enterprise, the rise of which reaches back into the centuries.

In the feudal system of the Middle Ages the masses served the lord and king in exchange for protection and subsistence. Then in the fifteenth and sixteenth centuries centralized control in western Europe was somewhat modified under the city-states and national governments. Excessive restrictions on the individual by the mercantilist system shifted attention from man-made law to natural law.

A profound influence on thinking was exerted by such men as Galileo, Kepler and Newton who discovered basic laws governing the physical world. A conviction took root that there existed a system of natural law which, free of undue government interference, would always lead to progress. It was the function of society, said William Godwin, not to make law but merely to interpret "that which the nature of things has already decreed."

Under this powerful new philosophy many laws restricting the freedom and the initiative of the individual were repealed. The conception of an economic world society was born. Men would be free to live and work where they liked.

In this country such conceptions found their golden opportunity. The inalienable rights of man were given eloquent expression in the Declaration of Independence. The human being was unfettered. In the nineteenth century the functions of government were to safeguard the individual, provide national defense and maintain a unified currency system. It was not a government function to engage in private enterprise or to regulate private business except for the prevention of monopoly. The great liberals of that day rightly believed that economic progress and human advancement could best be promoted by the so-called system of laissez faire, or non-interference.

Competition and the price system tended to maintain balance and ensure equity. Supply and demand determined output. If one industry began showing undue profits, new risk money moved into that industry and profits soon were reduced to normal. Inefficient, high-cost producers joined the ranks of enterprises which failed for inability to match price and quality. In varying degrees the private enterprise system prevailed in nearly every important country through the nineteenth century and the early decades of the twentieth century.

Despite the evidence that socialism would not provide a coherent national program, nor be directly responsive to the people's needs, there developed throughout the world in the decade of the nineteen thirties an expanding government control over the economic system. A new theory of economic organization gradually grew up in this country. The powers of government were invoked in the Roosevelt program for both recovery and economic control.

Such reform measures did not, however, bring about genuine business prosperity nor achieve stable economic conditions. Recovery in the spring and early summer of 1933 gave way to reaction in the autumn. Periodic advances and declines were recorded in the eighteen months beginning in mid-1934. The brief recovery of 1936-37 was pointed to as the fruits of a government-planned and controlled economy. But in 1938 production slid back to 1935 levels. From then onward the unemployment problem was severe until wartime production took up the slack.

A fleeting glance at the immense difficulties of government control of our huuge economy is provided in a war period. Obviously attempts at such control breeds inefficiency, suspicion, inequity, factional clashes, favoritism, graft, political jobs and the destruction of individual initiative and economic progress. Hybrid systems of socialism are failures.

History teaches that there must be one of two things: Communism, or statism, with its complete control, or democracy with its competitive system. Under democracy the government should confine itself to the elimination of monopoly and the preservation of free and open competition, and make certain that individual liberties are preserved. It should not engage in business.

Greedy, unwise taxation, in whatever form, helps to stop the free flow of venture capital, and this in turn puts an end to the dynamic economy essential to our high standard of living.

Growth in the cost of government is shocking. Many thoughtful men, astonished by the sensational rise of expenditures, wonder whether it is already too late to turn back.

George Washington was inaugurated in 1789. In the subsequent 152 years up to 1940 the government spent $167,000,000,000.

In four fiscal peace-time years alone, beginning in 1946, the government spent $177,000,000,000.

All Presidents through Franklin Roosevelt, in 156 years, took from the public in taxes $248,000,000,000. Two world wars and several smaller wars were fought.

In six years Harry Truman took from the public $260,000,000,000. This was $12,000,000,000 more than in all other Administrations of the past. It was reckoned the total of the Truman administration would be $320,000,000,000 by July 1, 1952. Even so, there was not enough tax money to pay current bills.

Most people have no conception of the staggering magnitude of government expenditures. For the calendar year 1951, Federal expenditures were nearly equal to all the wages and salaries of the more than 15,000,000 workers in all the factories and mines of the country. By comparison, in 1929 Federal expenditures represented only twenty percent of wages and salaries of the foregoing groups.

If state and local units are included, total governmental expenditures in 1951 were equal to about 57 percent of total wages and salaries of all persons, from the lowest paid worker to the highest paid executive, engaged in gainful non-Government pursuits.

With the upward surge of taxes, which increased eighteen times in two decades, the out-pouring of easy money brought increased waves of crime. Congressional crime investigations were a shocking revelation of the low state of public morality. In the darkening shadow of rising taxes came a mushrooming bureaucracy that threatened freedom.

Long ago grievances against the tyrannical King George III, as recorded by the Continental Congress in the Declaration of Independence, included: "He has erected a multitude of new offices, and sent hither swarms of officers to harass our people, and eat out their substance."

Today a swarming bureaucracy within our borders threatens our precious heritage of individual freedom. Total number of persons employed by Federal, state and local governments in July, 1951, not including the armed forces, was estimated at 6,356,000, a gain of 100 percent in twenty years, or four times the rate of population growth in the period. Most spectacular gains were in Federal civilian employment in the executive branch.

So bureaucracy became a widening wedge between the people and their government. Under a regime of bureaucracy, government is presided over by a group not elected by the people, a group that rules by directives instead of by laws. A spendthrift dynasty thus is created and perpetuates itself in power and its dead hand lays heavily upon individual freedom.

With all classes reeling under the tax burden and the oppressive bureaucracy, net return from business ventures, even under most favorable circumstances, was little more than that obtained from tax-exempt securities. The Government was taking the lion's share of winnings, while the investor, or risk bearer, absorbed the losses. This system was not unlike Karl Marx's platform of a century ago: Destroy the private enterprise system by imposing a heavy progressive or graduated income tax.

By the middle of 1952 many investors and corporate heads were deeply worried as to whether the immense tax grab of the Government would permit dividends sufficient to justify the risk of ownership. The following table mirrors federal taxes and dividends on 1951 earnings of a group of stocks. The stockholder's share of earnings is obtained by dividing the number of common shares into the total of common and preferred dividends.

	U.S. Taxes Per Share	Stockholder's Return Per Share
General Motors	$11.22	$4.15
U.S. Steel	15.24	3.97
U.S. Gypsum	20.60	7.34
International Harvester	8.72	2.42
Merck & Co.	3.37	.89
Union Carbide	5.71	2.50
Deere & Co.	19.97	5.47
Bethlehem Steel	18.38	4.68
American Cyanamid	11.67	4.12
Firestone	19.42	3.63
American Tobacco	8.88	4.59
Bendix Aviation	9.55	4.50
Carrier Corp.	8.03	2.12
Armco Steel	13.27	3.00
Douglas Aircraft	9.81	3.50
Allied Chemical	7.48	3.00
Goodrich	18.99	2.75
Canada Dry	2.03	.91
Owens-Illinois	10.28	4.00
Industrial Rayon	7.11	3.00
U.S. Rubber	40.38	8.96
North Pacific	9.84	2.25

Our government has become the most gigantic business on the face of the earth, reaching deep into the heart of innumerable enterprises, and sweeping into its orbit greater and greater controls over the acts of the individual. It has used the false cry of "Wall Street" to foster its socialistic schemes.

This audacious rise has been coincident with a political philosophy that business is "bad," that individual initiative requires more and more regulations, restrictions and prohibitions; that the merchant, manufacturer, farmer, laborer and physician must be regimented to save him from his own faulty thinking in a brave new world in which politics has become a major industry.

The Wall Street power myth is outdated. Not Wall Street, but Pennsylvania Avenue wields the financial power. In the public interest Congress should make clear the fact that government has in large measure taken over the business of finance and that unless such business is sent back where it belongs — to the banks and the free and open securities markets — then we have indeed embraced a new form of government, slyly and without popular vote, that may lead straight to complete socialism.

When vote-seekers are damning "Wall Street," they mean our banks and securities exchanges, our financia system, which is the finest ever created. By using the vague term of "Wall Street" they evade the necessity of a breakdown of facts. Such a breakdown in many instances would lay bare the true philosophy of the critic. And it would be a shock to a vast number of Americans who still placidly believe that we are preserving democracy in all its glory.

Once bureaucracy sits in final judgment over what new projects may be undertaken, then socialism has replaced democracy and that fact cannot be concealed in lofty phrases intended to draw an iron curtain around the separate parts of the capital and money markets.

Government attempts to control the lives of people and cut business to a pattern of politics have consistently failed down the centuries. In this country the profit motive is inherent in our system — it is the impelling, driving force that sends us ahead. The hour has arrived when the people must choose resolutely between the time-tested capitalistic system which shines with the achievement of progress, or some form of smothering collectivism that will retard economic growth and lower the standard of living.

To all students of the subject it is clear that to get back on the safe road of progress there must be a re-appraisal and revision of our peace-time federal tax structure. Sharp curtailment in the cost of government is an essential first step.

Even before the Korean outbreak in June of 1950, taxes had reached the danger zone, in the opinion of many experts. One of these, Colin Clark, the Australian economist, made an extensive study of the fiscal operations of many different countries. He came up with this finding: *The critical limit of taxation is 25 percent of national income.*

When that point is reached, he reported, governments resort to the easy way out by monetary devaluation, deficit financing, and inflation, rather than by increased taxation.

Taxes in the United States — federal, state, and local — reached that peril point by mid-year 1950 and sailed merrily onward.

Stepping briskly down the path of other nations in like situations, the United States embarked upon a deficit financing program. It was justified on the specious grounds that it would expand the economy (which always had voluntarily expanded), provide increased revenue, and fortify our fiscal position.

It is the age-old, discredited theory of spending one's way to solvency. It is the stage trappings of the demagogue and has been repudiated down the ages.

14: Wall Street Dilemma

Here and there left wing politicians still rant that Wall Street controls American finance. Yet there is indisputable evidence to the contrary. Far from exercising such control, the fact is that Wall Street has been steadily losing ground.

This loss of power is due not alone to the vast loan and banking business of the government. It is due in substantial measure to the fact that the trend of finance is westward and southward.

Today even the most loyal Wall Street boosters will tell you confidentially that the famous money lane may never regain its unchallenged strength of three decades ago.

Powerful economic and social forces have contributed immensely to the change. One significant influence was World War II which drew vast numbers of workers to the west and the south. Census reports clearly tell the story of the migrations. In California, Texas, Georgia and other states these workers established homes; their savings no longer poured through the sluggish channels of the east, but became new money, money searching for investment.

Bankers in the west and south awakened to the situation only when deposits began piling sky high. It was necessary to seek new enterprises; they began offering attractive loans for homes and commercial structures, and with low interest rates they beckoned to restless industries of the north and the east, many of which were increasingly bedeviled by the lords of labor.

At the same time a paternalistic government poured billions of dollars into the hinterland, not only for war plants, but to support farm prices, to promote rural electrification, and to pick up loans through the Reconstruction Finance Corporation and other lending agencies, loans which bankers, pursuing recognized policies of the trade, would not or could not properly make. Of this river of gold, precious little flowed back to Wall Street.

As we entered the second half of the century new plants, mills and factories were rising in areas distant from Wall Street which never before had been regarded as industrial regions. Steel mills had opened on the west coast; in Texas, of all places, chemical plants were sprawling across broad acres; New England had been losing textile mills to the sunny south. More and more southern produce that once went north for processing was now passing through the whirring machinery of southern mills.

In this conversion to industry some districts made rather sensational strides. In the Dallas area, for example, there are some sixteen hundred plants. Only a decade earlier there were far less than half this number, and they were smaller plants. Profits remain in the new industrial districts and go into plant expansion and bank loans for local development.

Some of the big New York banks do a local business, with branches scattered over the five boroughs. But others operate on a national scale, and as American banking power has surged westward these latter have felt the hot breath of competition. Aggressive banks of San Francisco, Chicago and Los Angeles, with new blood and imaginative leadership, have dashed out ahead in the race of the nation's ten largest, leaving several New York banks wondering what was taking place.

One yardstick of financial trends is the reserves held by member banks of the Federal Reserve System. In a period of ten years New York City member banks' reserves fell from 52 percent of the total to less than 27 percent.

Perhaps a more accurate index on financial volume is a factor which gauges checking activities. This is known as "debits to demand deposits." The grouping includes deposits of shopkeepers and other small businesses, but it is heavily weighted with the huge checks moving on the corporate and financing level, the New York Stock Exchange transactions, and the Wall Street underwriting activities.

This yardstick again showed the New York banks lagging behind the national trend. New York formerly accounted for an average of 45 percent of the nation's debits. By 1950 the figure had dropped to 36 percent.

In the same decade of comparison some cities were showing large increases in their checking deals. For example, Houston and Dallas snowballed their debit figures some 300 percent, and San Francisco 180 percent.

A study of bank deposits for a ten-year period reveals a similar lag in New York activities. New York's percentage of increase of 64 compares with Chicago's 106. Dallas showed a whopping 272, Houston 240, San Francisco 226, and Los Angeles 187. Reflecting the eastern dip, Philadelphia came up with 63, and Boston with 82.

Banking activities contribute to the prosperity of Wall Street, but the Street is more directly associated with stocks and bonds. Of course in bull markets such as that which began in the spring of 1949 Wall Street houses profit handsomely. But periodic bull markets are a poor gauge of long-term national basic trends. The cold fact is that the outlying stock exchanges have been jabbing constantly at the aging champion and some of them have shown greater percentage increases in trading volume.

Among these are the Los Angeles, San Francisco and Toronto exchanges. Like Chicago's Midwest Exchange (a consolidation of Chicago, St. Louis, Cleveland, Minneapolis-St. Paul exchanges) these outlying markets are hard-hitting teams that go after new business with marked determination and with no out-dated inhibitions.

They are particularly aggressive in lining up new listings; they do not depend solely upon local newspaper advertisements. The San Francisco exchange, as an example of dynamic western push, brought together stockholders and potential stockholders and took them on inspection tours of Pacific Coast industries which offered attractive investment opportunities. To round out this program, the investing public was given free courses on how to properly handle excess funds. The schoolroom was the floor of the exchange.

Chicago's hustling new combination of smaller exchanges constitutes somewhat of a threat to Wall Street in the years ahead. The leaders tell a convincing story to corporate heads whose securities are ripe for listing. The basic theme is that an exclusive Midwest listing means greater liquidity and a higher collateral value for shares, which in turn makes financing easier.

For many years Chicago has looked with envious eyes upon Wall Street. Chicago is the rail center, the agricultural capital, the hub of a vast industrial area, and its La Salle Street is a powerhouse of finance. It has been irksome to see business flow to New York that could and should be transacted in the centrally located second largest city. Deep in the hearts of Chicago business men is the confident belief that the Windy City, and not Wall Street or Washington, will eventually become the capital of finance. Each oncoming crop of young business men holds more firmly to that conviction. Colonel R. R. McCormick has preached the doctrine in his powerful Chicago Tribune for twenty years and millions in that broad area called "Chicagoland" have come to regard it as inevitable.

In chipping away at Wall Street, western firms have grown strong in the business of underwriting new issues. Today securities are being sold in every state in the Union; many of the smaller cities and towns offer ready markets. Hence it is no longer necessary for corporations to beat the well-worn path to Wall Street in quest of a bidder for their securities. More and more bidders are close at hand, and they know where they can market the stocks without facing east. To add to Wall Street's worries, in recent years insurance companies have scooped up many a big new issue floatation right under the startled noses of Wall Street's austere underwriting houses.

And that isn't all. Giant corporations, and some smaller ones, too, have long kept their central offices in New York, supposedly for the convenience of banking. In recent years stockholders have suspected that some of these corporate executives cling to New York for other reasons: Their vanity is flattered; they like the real or fancied prestige of playing the big time circuit.

But here again things are changing. A substantial number of these corporations, needled by brash but realistic western stockholders, are shifting headquarters to other sections, or delaying such shifts only until pressure becomes strong.

It is of course perfectly ridiculous for a corporation doing a vast percentage of its business in the west or south or mid-west to hole up in Wall Street when complete facilities are available at more central locations. Stockholders have complained that many of these Manhattan corporate executives become stuffed-shirts of narrow perspective; that they need to "get out into America" and toughen up to the new spirit of the south and the west. The extent of the corporate exodus will be up to stockholders.

Wall Street brokerage houses make no boasts of a shining record of achievement. Until recent years they displayed no deep-seated consciousness of the long-term welfare of the average investor. The single aim, in many cases, was simply to hold volume and collect trading commissions.

Lacking solid economic background, many brokers were rather ordinary men, surface thinkers who tried to determine the business trend in a somewhat hit and miss fashion. Too frequently they were more interested in the immediate market trend as created by powerful traders or pools than in basic economic conditions. In other words, the price swings of the day, not the long-term cycles, fastened their interest.

Yet for the most part these men were smug and haughty. Those serving rich clienteles were shocked at the very thought of publicly promoting new business, even to the extent of running a "tombstone" advertisement bearing the name and address. They dwelt in a pleasant, secure world; there was business enough to permit lush living and decent retirement.

In the 1920's when a new era of quick riches opened up, a pleasant patter of feet echoed in their board rooms. If they tried to exercise any knowledge of economics such effort was smothered in the spontaneous whoopee of buying orders. They kept margin requirements so low that anyone with a thousand dollars could buy ten thousand dollars worth of stock. Even when prices were high enough to have snow on them most brokerage houses went on encouraging new purchases by customers.

Then, as might be expected, they were stunned by the 1929 debacle, for economic reality had been ignored. Not only were they shocked (and many lost heavily on their own speculations) but they were virtually bankrupt of ideas for meeting the situation.

Whipped, depressed, fearful of the next move by the howling crowd of New Deal left-wingers who were out for blood, they clammed up, and did not fight back even when unfairly put upon; they devoted themselves to cutting payrolls, closing branch offices, and adjusting to the long years of 400,000-share days, commissions from which had to be spread out among the 600 member firms of the New York Stock Exchange, 433 of whom are in New York City.

By loss of public confidence and loss of customers, securities brokers paid heavily for their blundering stupidity and their lack of conception of public welfare.

In the lush days they had hired glib young men, personality boys, who were known as customers men. Most of them had little basic knowledge of investment, or even of judicious speculation. They learned the jargon, parroted the words of investment service sheets, and tossed off a line that sounded enchanting to the crowds with gambling money.

Today the brokerage fraternity is reformed, streamlined, and disciplined. Great progress has been made toward adjusting the business to a realistic basis. This is being done as a matter of self-preservation; brokers realize that when customers lose their money they are no longer customers.

Yet a few houses will still recommend the purchase of a stock, usually with good reason, and then forget any further responsibility; the customer frequently carries that stock, or a group of stocks, until the bottom drops out. In other words, such houses do not watch the customer's portfolio and try earnestly to get him out at a propitious time. Instead they say, in effect, "now you're in and you're on your own."

Until a more systematic follow-up on the securities of the individual customer has been developed by all brokerage houses they are failing in their full responsibility to the customer. The man who handles the public's money should have more to sell than personality; he should render a service beyond that of executing an order which one broker can do about as well as another. He should strive to preserve the capital of the customer and to see to it, not that he gets rich on unbridled speculation, but that he receives a fair return on his money as one of the owners of American industry.

In the dark and barren days of the 1930's brokers sat around dreaming of lusher times when the big board memberships were selling, not for $25,000, but for $600,000. And while they dreamed, their old customers and potential new customers were pouring what excess funds they had into insurance, annuities, real estate, government bonds — anything but common stocks.

In that period strange stories of the lack of faith of broker with customer were creeping over the grapevine. A typical one concerned a group of men who headed half a dozen New York brokerage houses. It was reported that in the late 'twenties they met at a swanky golf club on week-ends and compared notes. If they found their books heavily laden with long trades in a particular stock they would thereupon agree to recommend the sale of that stock on the following Monday morning. And, so the story went, they would start things off with personal short sales before advising customers to sell. Then by buying at the bottom of the break they would thus enjoy a two-way ride.

It is very doubtful that the story is true; in any case, it could not happen under the tight laws of today. But true or false, the tale was convincing to the trading public, and, like other exaggerations, it was trumpeted by the pinkos and left-wing planners. To the uninitiated it explained those Monday morning breaks in prices. Yet the fact is that statistics covering a long period of years showed that markets usually were lower on Monday and higher on Friday for entirely different reasons.

Streamlined, chastened by the new rigid laws, and fearful lest an artificial condition might build up to another crash that would invite legislative fury, the brokerage fraternity gave a better account of itself as the bull market, based on huge corporate earnings and government inflationary policies, plowed through the years of 1950 and 1951. The sharp rise chronicled the lustiest bull market in twenty-one years.

To those familiar with the stormy markets of the late 'twenties the contrast was very pronounced. Even in the shock of war, markets behaved well. But of course there were no pools in operation, whooping it up with splendid disregard of public rights. So the great trading floor was orderly, as traders watched the magnified ticker tape flickering across the screens at the four corners of the spacious hall. The rejuvenated Bull was of an entirely different pedigree from the Bull of the roaring 'twenties. He was not trailed by a rabble of cab drivers, barbers, headwaiters, and chorus girls trying to make a quick killing on a shoestring.

That type of thin-margin speculators had been banished by the provision calling for a margin of 50 percent of the purchase price, which was raised to 75 percent in January of 1951, and which is one of the soundest measures ever applied to security trading. The higher the margin the greater is the market's stability.

Nor was the market bedeviled by the reckless raids of short-sellers. Under a rule of the Securities and Exchange Commission short sales may be made only on the "up tick," that is, when the stock has risen at least an eighth of a point after the short-sale order is placed. That, too, is a healthy, constructive measure in the interest of the investor.

Another curious contrast was found in the fact that most purchasers of stock, instead of being bent on making a quick killing, were more interested in taking advantage of large dividend returns. Tastes generally ran to "blue chip" stocks, with long records of good earnings.

But of course none of the restrictions helpful to the public could keep fools from losing their money if they were determined to do so. The consoling fact, however, was that there were fewer of the tin-horn gambling type reaching for quick profits, the same type that yell loudest when hurt by their own indiscretions.

On the other hand, there was developing a broadscale owner-

ship of American industries by large numbers of responsible permanent investors which is undeniably helpful in maintaining the
American form of democracy. Brokers are increasingly conscious
of that fact, and many are spending money to advance the doctrine.

In recent years a most heartening development, from a public
welfare standpoint, was the strong leadership of a few large brokerage houses in revising the philosophy of the broker-customer relationship. To Charles E. Merrill must go much of the credit for this new
conception of putting the customer's interest first.

Merrill heads the largest stock and commodity brokerage house,
a combination of a number of houses brought together after the 1929
crash. It is known as Merrill Lynch, Pierce, Fenner & Beane, but
because of its many partners and its far-flung operations the trade
calls it "We, the People" or just plain "We."

Two basic problems convinced Merrill that something should
be done. One was the disrepute of brokerage houses with the public;
the other was the dwindling number of wealthy investors and professional traders.

To remedy the situation Merrill set out to interest the expanding
middle class in securities as a medium of permanent investment, and
at the same time to explain the complicated machinery of investment.
He visualized a long-range public relations and display advertising
campaign, an important aim of which was to heal the wounds dating
from the disreputable 'twenties.

It is a startling departure when a single brokerage house spends
up to $1,500,000 a year for research, investment booklets for custom-
ers, and such-like educational publicity. Cynics in the fraternity
stood on the sidelines awaiting an anticipated dismal failure of the
daring plan. But instead they saw the brisk tactics and lavish expenditures of the house of Merrill pay off handsomely.

Perhaps, reasoned some brokers, there may be something to
this implied slogan that the customer is king. In any case, several
other large houses decided to adopt similar programs. They set up
research departments really worthy of the name, and issued sound
statistical documents, and began telling the story of judicious investment in newspapers, magazines and on the radio.

Even the more slowly-moving policy-makers of the New York
Stock Exchange at length decided that something should be done to
interest Main Street in the wares of Wall Street. Accordingly, an
$800,000 a year fund was projected for the purpose of explaining to
investors the basic role of the stock market. A good job is being done.

But to date the surface has only been scratched. Brokerage houses now realize that all other businesses, to survive, are compelled to render better and better service. They recognize that they have a new and greater responsibility in these changing times. To retain public confidence they must render superior service to the customer, and at the same time fight their greatest enemy, which is extreme run-away markets.

All brokerage houses might well set aside a larger percentage of gross income to be used in the public interest, in research and basic investment education. In light of Wall Street's dwindling power as a center of finance, New York houses should recognize the urgency of the situation and not be blinded by any transitory periods of affluence due to special conditions of war or inflation.

Outlying exchanges will bid stronger and stronger for the investor's business. But even this erosion is hardly less serious than the amazing growth of investment companies. Wall Street has watched with surprise the rise and expansion of these "mutual funds" organizations, whose shares for the most part are sold direct to the investor. They represent a tremendous loss of business to member firms of the New York Stock Exchange.

The "mutuals" have grown because they have inspired the confidence of the public and offered a service which the brokerage houses, fenced in with tradition, have failed to offer.

If there is to be a new conception of widespread public ownership of American industry the stock broker must play a more important role. To perform maximum service, the brokerage house should have its own capable research organization. It should insist that the customer make known his entire list of investments. These should be reviewed at frequent periods, not simply with an eye to new commissions, but with a determination to protect the customer's interests. Changes should be recommended only on the basis of clearly supporting evidence. At the end of each year a complete report should reveal to the customer how good, mediocre, or bad the service had been, compared with the market as a whole.

Thus business would drift to those houses performing a superior service to the investing public, and incompetents would fall by the wayside, just as they do in other lines of business. If there were too many houses reaching for quick commissions, the number would be reduced by competition, in the public interest.

It is highly probable that the splendid progress of better public service will continue.

15: Streamlining Small Investors

In towns and cities across the land many bright young men, alight with enthusiasm, are ringing doorbells and selling shares in mutual investment funds to householders with a yearning to become small capitalists.

Success of the continuous drive by more than 10,000 salesmen is mirrored in the almost breathless post-war rise of these funds. At the beginning of 1952 net assets of the biggest 103 companies exceeded $3,000,000,000. This was an increase of 170 percent since 1945.

Nor has the field been more than scratched, declare the confident leaders of this new investment phenomenon. They find their best potential market in that huge group of men and women with annual incomes of from $4,500 to $6,000.

To make sure that none is overlooked, some promoters of the funds advertise in labor and foreign language newspapers and in overseas magazines. Others carry on direct mail campaigns that spill out into foreign lands; still others put on puppet shows and set up exhibits at state fairs.

Smartest single move of recent times was the deal of the Mutual Fund Institute with the National Federation of Women's Clubs. The Federation finally agreed to place the subject of mutual funds on its study list for a half million members.

Three distinct advantages are offered to the mutual fund investor. One is wide diversification of holdings; another is professional investment management, and a third it continuous supervision.

Funds are tailored to any taste. You may buy shares in a fund made up solely of common stocks, or one with bonds only, or one with stocks and bonds. There are other funds with only bank and insurance stocks, or oils, or chemicals; and if one feels real frisky with his money he may put it into a fund which speculates in commodity futures markets. Thus the spirited sales technique overlooks no one with surplus cash.

Bankers have sometimes raised a brow at the rapidity of growth which has occurred in a period of prosperity, a period in which funds were not put to any harsh test. Yet it is admitted that shareholders are given the fullest possible information and are safeguarded by stout laws and regulations.

If you were to seek your broker's opinion as to the advantages of such investments, he might look at you sadly and shake his head, for he is quite conscious of the fact that a substantial part of this big flow of money is neatly channeled around stock exchange houses.

Of course a number of New York Stock Exchange members now handle mutual shares and likewise profit from direct brokerage transactions for the investment companies. But the many non-participating houses are left out in the cold.

Since stock brokerage prosperity rises and falls with economic cycles, partners in many houses view with dismay the sensational growth of the funds and they ponder the threat in those years when a small volume of public trade must be divided among many. "Splitting the cherry," this was called in the skimpy 1930's.

Brokers clearly recognize a major trend in the economy which is gradually transferring into the hands of investment institutions of various kinds a growing percentage of the ownership of leading American corporations.

This process, they hear an officer of the National Association of Investment Companies say, "will be even more accelerated in the immediate future. The investment company is, of course, participating in this movement . . . and is here to stay."

It is also especially painful to observe large private off-'change transactions by mutual funds, some blocks of securities totaling 50,000 or more shares at a clip. The implication is not heartening to many brokers.

Long ago investment trusts made their appearance in England and Scotland. Before the turn of the century they had dug deep into the economy. Their shares, representing wide diversification of common and preferred stocks, were held by all classes of investors.

It was not until after World War I that the idea took hold in earnest in this country. Then it mushroomed into proportions that seemed hideous after the historic crash. Some 700 companies of various types had more than seven billion dollars of assets in 1929.

In most instances these assets shrunk in proportion to the general market decline; there were consolidations, liquidations, retiring of shares and other emergency measures. When it was all over the public looked upon investment companies with a jaundiced eye. Yet a considerable number of the companies gave a reasonably good accounting of their stewardship.

Plainly the investment companies, like the stock exchanges, required regulation in the public interest. Their mistakes and abuses were spot-lighted in a comprehensive study by the Securities and Exchange Commission. Then they were placed under the supervisory regulation of SEC by the Investment Company Act of 1940.

While this act brought order out of chaos and afforded substantial public protection, some congressmen argue that there still are chinks in the law that need plugging. Even so, in its broader aspects the law provides sharp supervision of types of securities purchased, loans, underwriting, and management. It put an end to short selling and margin trading by investment companies.

In this expanding field where the little man may buy a diversified stake in American industry there are two types of companies: the so-called open-end or mutual fund companies, and the closed-end companies. The distinction is simple. The open-end companies have no fixed capitalization. They are constantly offering their shares to buyers. Since the number of shares outstanding changes from day to day the term "open-end" is fairly descriptive.

Closed-end companies are management companies. Their securities are bought and sold on the stock exchanges or over-the-counter, the same as the average stock. There are two specific groups of the closed-end companies, each recognized by the Investment Company Act. One group includes corporations which have large interests in particular situations or industries. The other, and much larger group of closed-end companies, invest their funds in a broad and diversified list of securities.

Many of these closed-end companies stood up under severe tests during the strenuous period of recovery and stabilization which began in 1936. In recent years they have achieved a high degree of uniformity of practices. Some have been strikingly aggressive in seeking out investment opportunities. But most of them lean toward the time-tested, conventional investment procedures and diversify their holdings widely among leading securities in basic industries.

Success of these companies rests upon good management. Good management means the ability to increase net assets faster than the market average in a bull period, and to prevent asset shrinking as rapidly as the average during a declining market period.

Some of these closed-end companies have achieved much better than average results. Among the straight management companies with diversified holdings the deviation from the average in recent years has been relatively moderate.

It is the open-end or mutual fund companies which, rightly or wrongly, inspire in many brokers a bleak philosophy of the future and make them wonder whether there will be business enough for all present member houses of exchanges if current trends continue.

Registered with SEC are 118 open-end companies, as against 83 closed-end companies. For the 98 open-end or mutual fund companies included in its membership, the National Association of Investment Companies showed total net assets of well over $2,500,000,000 at the end of 1950. Total net assets of 38 closed-end member companies are nearly $1,000,000,000.

Member companies of the association of both types had nearly 1,500,000 shareholders and distributed more than $200,000,000 in dividends in a year. Statistics on growth in the past ten years are imposing.

Sponsors of the open-end investment companies set forth many reasons for the persistent growth. High taxes have forced the very wealthy and many upper-bracket executives out of common stocks and into tax-exempt bonds. A new class of investors — rich farmers, high wage earners, professional and small business men — must carry the slack in common stocks, which are the basis of venture capital. The prodigious growth of this new prosperous class is shown in Federal Reserve Board studies.

The little investor needs investment advice just as he needs legal and medical advice. Mutual funds, it is contended, provide this guidance and, like insurance, bring the magic of averages to the service of the millions. The man with a few hundred dollars obtains essentially the same type of widely diversified stock ownership and supervision as the man of great wealth. He has protection from dangers that he would be unable to brave alone.

Like the man of wealth, the little investor, whose average stake in mutual funds is less than $3,000, worries about the drift of government and strives to preserve his savings in what he fears is a rising tide of socialism. He likes the investment companies because, as they point out to him, they are as a group one of the largest holders of common stocks; their proxies "have influence on management policies of corporations where he alone would have none." He likes the feeling that the law requires redemption of his shares on demand.

But the little man is not alone the ultimate aim of the mutual funds managers. They point out that old-line institutions, educational endowments, charitable and religious funds, pension and retirement funds, and even ordinary trust funds have become less and less able to meet their obligations by ownership of high grade bonds. They have been forced to seek partial relief in common stocks.

States have been lifting restrictions to permit trustees, and in some cases insurance companies, to purchase a reasonable percentage of common stock. The large endowments and trust institutions can afford trained staffs to select their common stocks. But the smaller ones cannot do so, and consequently more and more of them are turning to investment company securities.

In tapping all these new wells of investment capital, and particularly those of the small investors, the mutual fund sponsors claim they not only are building a broad base of industry ownership, but they are helping to stop the sweep of state socialism. Moreover, it is claimed their huge holdings help to stabilize markets.

Briefly, here is how they view the future — to the anxiety of many a stock broker: "Mutual fund investment companies are capable of indefinite expansion. If the man in the street maintains his confidence, they may in time become the major institutional medium for the equity ownership of American industry."

Critics grant that most of these open-end "investors' cooperatives," as some like to be called, are headed by men of high integrity and superior ability. But they object to certain claims and certain methods of promotion.

They don't like, for example, what they call the assumption by mutual funds that the small American investor is too dumb to understand basic investment problems and that therefore he must be streamlined to a pattern.

Nor do they like overly-aggressive sales policies which sometimes create the impression that miracles may be expected from investment company management. It would seem that they have a point here, for it became necessary for SEC on October 1, 1950, to impose upon open-end companies new regulations with respect to sales literature.

Vigorous sales efforts have indeed accounted for growth, rather than a spontaneous rush by small investors to buy shares. The vast majority of shares are sold by dealers in the unlisted securities market. It is estimated that such sales represent one quarter of the total business of these dealers.

Critics say the shares should be sold for what they are, that the wares should not be misbranded as panaceas for all financial ills nor as the equivalent in safety of a savings bank account. Investors should have a full understanding of the risks, which are always present in equity investments. The agent of an investment company should be compelled to observe the highest standards of integrity, for he is not the bearer of a magician's wand.

It is conceded by critics that wide diversification and supervision are tremendous advantages in any investment program. Nor do they belittle the findings of the Investment Companies Committee of the Investment Bankers Association of America. At the thirty-eighth annual convention this committee reported: "There is no record, for instance, of an open-end or mutual fund ever having interrupted its dividend payments."

But the critics point out that the rather astonishing growth has come in a period of rising markets, and that "there is nothing a bull market won't cure."

Frequently the question is asked as to what would happen to the open-end companies in a tremendous liquidating movement with vast numbers of shareholders demanding redemption. First, the government would probably halt any such movement before it reached the destructive proportions of the 1929-32 collapse. Secondly, under section 22-E of the law, SEC could suspend redemption of shares in an emergency.

By far the most logical complaint of critics is the original "loading" charge made on the purchase of open-end shares. These premiums have averaged around 7½ to 8 per cent over a period of years, according to a comprehensive study by one of the largest investment advisory services. Some run as high as 9.6 and others lower than 8 percent. A few have no loading charge. Said this review:

"Closed-end company stocks selling at discounts could logically be expected to produce a larger return than open-end company shares because of the lower initial cost." The usual premium does not go into the fund but is divided between the distributor and the dealer, or salesman. The commission received by the dealer is far more than the commission a dealer would receive for handling a similar transaction involving a listed security.

Mutual funds have without doubt tapped many new pools of capital (some critics call them puddles) that have helped to spread ownership in American industry. They point proudly to a survey covering a three-year period. This showed that 31 percent of the new capital they raised came from states along the North Atlantic seaboard. Oddly enough, in the same period 69 per cent of the business on the New York Stock Exchange came from the North Atlantic seaboard and only 31 percent from all other areas.

Hence it is argued that shares of the open-end companies are owned in large part by new investors who have not purchased securities on the New York Stock Exchange. In this very fact nervous brokers visualize a growing loss of business as these investors become more affluent and as vast numbers of additional investors turn their assets to the mutual funds.

As to the claim of mutual funds that they create abundant new venture capital there is some disagreement. It is true, however, that they frequently absorb the extra shares offered stockholders by a corporation, shares that an individual investor is not always in a position to accept.

On one point there seems to be agreement. The investment companies are indeed here to stay. And in the words of one authority, if they maintain their astonishing rate of growth the public responsibility of their managers will become almost frightening.

In trying to balance advantages against disadvantages of mutual funds, neutral authorities seem to feel that for many small investors these funds serve a worthwhile purpose. They point to the particularly favorable feature of redemption. Trusts will redeem their shares on request, ordinarily at the net asset value.

They concede that the loading charge is greater than that incurred under direct investment methods; but they stress the fact that the investor is, after all, buying a service of supervision which he himself usually is unable to properly perform. Even if he were capable, the time he spent at the task would have some value.

It seems to be the consensus among neutral experts that for small sums, say up to $15,000, the mutual funds offer an attraction. But as a rule a fund of $25,000 or more may be invested directly with the advice of competent investment counsel for less cost than the average investment trust fees and expenses.

Few small investors who trade in stocks are able to obtain results over a long period of time comparable to the average performance of American investment trusts.

Whether the small investor turns to mutual funds or to closed-end trusts, he will be well advised to choose his company most carefully. A comprehensive study from the investor's point of view has been made by the American Institute for Economic Research of Great Barrington, Mass. The booklet, entitled "Investment Trusts and Funds," classifies the various investment trusts, and is sold for one dollar. Other literature is available at reference libraries.

Smart investors will spend a little time reading up before buying the wares of the first salesman of shares who happens along.

6: You and Your Money

It is perfectly astonishing, said a leading economist, how people struggle to accumulate money and then give relatively little thought to its safe investment.

Yet there never was a time when abundant investment information was so readily available. This very abundance seems to bewilder the average investor. He is awed by imposing statistical tables and confused by the pontifical market jargon of some investment service experts, writers who strive to hedge their opinions in a cloud of words.

In the end most investors simply turn to others for advice. Certainly there is no objection to such a course, for all investors cannot hope to become financial experts. But all investors, regardless of confidence in their advisers, can and should study closely the particular investments into which they are drawn. Such intelligent effort will reward them over a period of years. Blind faith has no place in the realistic field of investment.

Thousands of helping hands are ready to assist you in the investment of your funds. A few hot little hands still reach out from strange nooks and crannies, but they find the pickings small. Fortunately for the public, most of the tipsters and tricksters who infested the financial districts in the 'twenties have been outlawed.

Under the Investment Advisers Act of 1940, persons engaged for compensation in the business of advising on securities must register with the Securities and Exchange Commission. Thus fraud and deceit are made difficult. Investment advisers must disclose the nature of their interest in transactions for clients. The law prohibits profit-sharing deals and other free and easy policies of former times by which the innocent frequently were trimmed.

In its annual report published in May of 1951 the S.E.C. showed 1,044 registrations. Of this number 242 registered advisers supervised investments on the basis of the individual client's needs. The services of 335 others were rendered chiefly through publications of different types. Registered also as brokers and dealers were 232 investment advisers. The remainder offered various combinations of services.

Most of these registered advisers are men of good reputation. But the law is weak in some respects. If a man has a clean legal record he may register even though he be wholly unqualified for such work, where the public welfare is involved. For example, one applicant for registration frankly stated that it was his intent to chart the course of stock prices by the moon and the stars. Legally there was no way to bar him, aside from endless technical delays.

Another gentleman, Frederick N. Goldsmith, whose financial service bore his name, suddenly found his registration revoked. He had led his clients to believe he was a skilled investment adviser, but the Commission sorrowfully reports that his findings "were fraudulent and reckless," for they were "admittedly based in part on the comic strips in which he believed there existed a code which, interpreted by him, would reflect future movements of securities."

Only an alert and aggressive legal staff at S.E.C. prevents endless irregularities under the broad privileges accorded by the act.

Rules for prudent investment of your funds are almost as numerous as investment experts. But certain fundamentals are self-evident.

First of all, any man with family responsibilities should have a life insurance program. In recent years of high government debt and a shrinking dollar the argument frequently was heard that your insurance dollar may be worth but ten or fifteen cents in purchasing power by the time it reaches the beneficiaries. Even such a dismal possibility as that could hardly justify the absence of a protective insurance program.

Next to insurance and a home, one should have a modest savings account for emergency purposes. Some funds should go into high grade bonds, and as additional capital is available it should, for purposes of larger income return, be invested in preferred stocks, and carefully selected common stocks.

Many people of substantial means turn their investment problems to others on a fixed fee basis. Numerous large banks now maintain extensive research staffs in trust departments, with capable investment advisory committees. The service charge generally by such banks is one-half of one percent of the total fund handled, with a minimum charge of $250 a year. Thus a fund of $100,000 would involve an annual fee of $500. The bank suggests changes in the portfolio but it acts only on approval of the client, unless otherwise instructed. Incidentally, it costs no more to select a bank with a genuinely capable investment staff.

Other people of substantial means engage a recognized investment adviser to guide them. Still others use the facilities of large investment publication services, which for an additional fee will set up a balanced portfolio and recommend changes as conditions warrant.

Perhaps the largest number of investors depend upon the advice of their brokers. This is a satisfactory arrangement if the brokerage house has a reputation for intelligent and conservative policies and maintains a research staff worthy of the name. However, if an investor finds himself being taken in and out of the market at very frequent intervals, he would be well advised to change houses, for he has left the field of judicious long-term investment and has become a short-term speculator whose thin profits are likely to vanish in commissions on trades.

As public ownership of corporate securities expands, a growing number of investors strive to do their own thinking. This encouraging trend is evidenced by the increased circulations of most of the major financial services, such as Moody, Standard & Poor's, Fitch, Babson, Alexander Hamilton Institute, and the like. These and a number of other respected services are worth the money, if only for the comprehensive statistical material provided.

For those whose investment funds are not large enough to justify subscription, such investment publications are available free at most brokerage offices, banks, and at some libraries. Available also at modest cost are several thoughtful investment magazines. Then, too, a number of large banks issue monthly business and economic bulletins which may be had free. Some of them, like the *Business Bulletin* of The Cleveland Trust Company, and the *New England Letter* of The First National Bank of Boston, are especially useful as guides to current and future business trends.

It cannot be too strongly stressed that every investor in securities should read and think. He has the greatest interest in preservation of his funds. He should read regularly at least one financial publication or investment service report. In the course of a few months many of the mysteries surrounding sound investment will begin to clarify; he will find himself in tune with conditions; he will anticipate events and not be caught napping when sweeping economic changes occur.

Even the mentally lazy can discipline themselves to half an hour of such reading and thought each day. It is an excellent type of investment insurance. Unless an investor is equipped to argue a point intelligently with his broker or other adviser he is guilty of neglect and should not be surprised at an occasional beating in the market. Broker, banker and investment adviser, consciously or unconsciously, seem to have more respect for the informed investor and tend to exercise superior care in making recommendations.

The ability of your broker, banker, investment adviser, or investment service should be judged not solely on what is accomplished in a bull market, when most stocks are rising, but on what is achieved by way of preserving your capital in a bear market. Therein lies the major test.

It is the policy of some investment services to boast in their publications of how certain stocks previously recommended have risen to great heights. Investors should not be misled by such pounding of the drums. A study of ALL the recommended "buys" of such boastful services often shows an equal number of faulty predictions.

When a stock is recommended for purchase, by whatever source, its entire background should be studied before a decision is made. What is the stock's position in its industry? How did it act in the dismal 1929-33 period? What is its record of growth and its future prospect? For how many consecutive years has it paid a cash dividend? How did its earnings hold up during the worst depression years? All such information is readily available and should be checked and weighed with care.

After studying the broad subject of investment over a period of thirty years, this writer is convinced that common stocks of good American corporations, purchased at opportune times and held over a period of years, offer splendid opportunity for liberal income and capital enhancement.

This statement is, of course, based on the assumption that we maintain our present form of government and do not drift deeper into a socialistic or welfare state.

In this democracy of ours stock ownership is one of the most completely democratic institutions to be found anywhere. In many lands, by reason of socialistic and police state restrictions, such privilege is denied or rigidly restricted. In some countries the citizens are compelled, by taxation, to provide capital for government-owned corporations whether they like it or not. Yet they are denied the right to participate proportionately in any profits.

It is estimated that some 15 million Americans own corporation stocks. In May of 1951 a Saginaw, Michigan couple purchased seven shares of American Telephone & Telegraph Company and became that corporation's millionth shareholder. AT&T has paid a dividend every year, in good times and bad, since 1881. And no single stockholder owns ½ of 1 percent of the corporation.

In the giant U. S. Steel Corporation, with a quarter of a million stockholders, no one person holds as much as 3/10 of 1 percent of either preferred or common stock; and the vast majority of General Motors' half-million shareholders are people of modest income.

In fact, federal income studies show that about one-third of all dividend payments on common stocks go to persons with yearly incomes of less than $5,000.

Certain it is that average investors are mainly those of moderate resources — professional men and women, the farmer, business men and women, and thrifty wage-earners who, after personal emergency reserves are provided for, seek to increase their incomes by thoughtful investment of idle funds.

As political agitation for socialistic laws abates, the junior securities of corporations rise in popularity, stimulated by a rise in public confidence. There have been periods of agitation in the past two decades when stocks remained substantially below their true values.

In 1950 and 1951 common stocks of corporations began to be purchased in volume by trust funds, set up for private estates, educational institutions, and pension reserves. In many instances such trust funds were able to obtain two or even three times the return from dividend yields that had been obtained on government bonds and municipal bonds. To permit such funds to gain a fair and realistic return more State laws limiting trust investments were being relaxed.

By the middle of 1951 pension funds set up by U. S. industry and its employes already held reserves estimated at nearly 11 billion dollars. Some able authorities believe that, as new pension plans come into the field and reserves keep building up, these funds soon will be increasing at a rate of around 3 billion dollars a year.

It is also estimated that at least 10 percent of this addition to pension funds will be invested in common stocks. Thus the future

impact of pension money alone on common stocks could be significant. Such investment would tend to stabilize markets and reduce
the extent of price swings in periods of uncertainty. And as price
swings are tempered, the true merit of common stocks as long-range
investments should be more clearly realized.

Trustees for pension funds and other trusts lean heavily on the
"blue chip" class of stocks. This emphasis on gilt-edged securities
raises in the minds of some experts the question of where small,
growing concerns will be able to get venture capital. It would be
reasonable to conclude, however, that with a financially sound government, free of extreme socialistic tendencies, and with an economy
broadening to an extent commensurate with increased population, the
venture capital problem should be readily solved.

A New York brokerage house made a study to determine the
favorite stocks of investment trusts. It was found, of course, that a
high percentage of their holdings were in the top strata securities.
The favorite twenty-five as held by these trusts were shown as follows:

Company	Market Value (Millions)	Number of Trusts Holding
Gulf Oil	$30.8	67
International Paper	29.8	49
Continental Oil	27.3	64
Amerada	27.0	24
DuPont	24.2	55
Texas Company	23.3	50
General Motors	22.2	69
General Electric	21.3	65
Standard Oil (N.J.)	19.9	59
Kennecott Copper	19.8	62
Union Carbide	19.2	52
Sears, Roebuck	19.0	48
Goodrich	18.9	39
Montgomery Ward	18.8	59
Westinghouse Electric	18.1	59
Chrysler	17.3	47
Phillips Petroleum	17.2	55
Standard Oil Indiana	16.7	46
North American Co.	15.7	35
Standard Oil Calif.	15.1	35
Int'l. Business Machine	14.2	28
United Gas	14.1	52
Dow Chemical	13.9	35
Middle South Utilities	13.6	46
Celanese Corp.	13.4	40

In light of their record over the years, few people dare impinge
the character of blue chips; and it is for that very reason that trustees
of various funds are inclined to favor the gilded shares. When such

securities actually go bad, most everything else is hitting the bumps and alibis are not difficult to come by.

Records of many common stocks reflect extraordinary stability of earnings in good times and bad over long periods of years. At the beginning of 1951 there were 281 common stocks listed on the New York Stock Exchange which had paid cash dividends every year for from 20 to 102 years. The average dividend yield on these stocks was 6 percent. Shrewd investors seeking stable, liberal return rather than quick price enhancement favor "antiques," that is, stocks with long unbroken dividend records, stocks that held up better than the market as a whole in the distressing early 'thirties, a period of economic severity that is unlikely to be repeated under the strengthened laws governing new security issues, security trading, and commercial and investment banking.

A list of "antiques" can be obtained from the New York Stock Exchange or from any member firm. For the investor unfamiliar with common stocks, who is entering that field of investment, a careful study of such long-time dividend payers should be helpful. Risk of ownership is always present in whatever investment is made, but there are many needless risks that can be avoided if one holds determinedly to judicious policies. One such policy is never to over-buy. It is unwise for the small investor to saddle himself with debit balances by making purchases on margin. If your funds are sufficient to buy but fifty shares of a stock, do not buy an extra fifty and later find yourself pressed for more margin in a falling market. Pay for what you buy when you buy it; order the stock out, and put the certificate in a safe deposit box with insurance policies and other valuable papers.

A study of all dividend-paying common stocks regularly traded on the New York Stock Exchange shows the close relationship between prices and dividend yields.

For the decade 1901-1910, common stocks sold on the average of 20.1 times their dividends. For the next decade the ratio averaged only 15.2 times dividends. Despite wide price fluctuations in certain periods of the past thirty years, the ratio by decades has remained fairly constant. For 1921-1930 it averaged 16.6 times. For 1931-1940 the average was 16.9 times; and for 1941-1950 it was 16.4 times.

For the entire period of 50 years, dividend-paying common stocks sold on the average of 16.9 times their dividends. This compared with a figure of 16.2 times in April of 1951 during a bull market period.

Even such mad speculative orgies as that which took place in the late 'twenties can disturb but temporarily the basic pattern of common stock values. Such values are tied to the industrial growth of the country. This industrial growth is somewhat surprising when present-day corporate asset comparisons are made, for instance, with the boom days of the 'twenties.

Analysis of corporate reports covering 1950 showed that at least twenty-three companies had total listed assets of a billion dollars or more. Thirty-six other companies had listed assets of at least half a billion dollars. Nor do these groups include banks and insurance companies whose assets are largely owned by others.

Some investors prefer to buy common stocks in the giant corporations on the theory that since they are deeply enrooted in the economy there is an added element of safety. Conditions change with progress, however, and in the case of railroads, for example, the asset growth has not been so imposing.

Companies with listed assets of a billion dollars or more in 1951 included the following:

Company	Latest Assets (in billions)	1929 Assets (in billions)
American Tel & Tel	11.6	4,228
Standard Oil of Jersey	4.2	1,767
General Motors	3.4	1,324
U. S. Steel	2.8	2,286
N. Y. Central Railroad	2.5	1,606
Pennsylvania Railroad	2.3	2,078
Southern Pacific	1.9	2,278
Canadian Pacific	1.8	1,339
Standard Oil of Indiana	1.6	697
Consolidated Edison	1.6	1,171
Socony-Vacuum	1.6	708
duPont de Nemours	1.5	497
Texas Company	1.4	312
Atchison, Topeka & Santa Fe	1.4	1,262
Gulf Oil	1.3	431
Bethlehem Steel	1.3	801
General Electric	1.3	492
Pacific Gas & Electric	1.2	428
Baltimore & Ohio	1.2	1,110
Union Pacific	1.2	1,195
CIT Financial Corp.	1.2	209
Standard Oil of Calif.	1.2	605
Sears, Roebuck	1.0	252

Other companies showing assets of more than half a billion dollars included the following, and the two groups constitute the backbone of the nation's economy, producing as they do a vast portion of such vital items as fuel, steel, power, chemicals and communications, and providing the vast network of railroads.

Company	Latest Assets	1929 Assets
	(in millions)	
Cities Service	936	1,090
Humble Oil & Refining	936	240
Commonwealth Edison	927	376
Union Carbide & Carbon	869	307
Northern Pacific	868	866
Chesapeake & Ohio	863	550
Great Northern	858	852
American Gas & Electric	827	148
Westinghouse Electric	800	254
Sinclair Oil	799	401
Commercial Credit	799	40
International Harvester	749	384
Chrysler Corp.	744	210
Shell Oil	723	486
Southern Railway	721	692
Creole Petroleum	719	48
Public Service Elec. & Gas	705	321
Anaconda Copper	699	681
Chicago, Burlington	694	712
Montgomery Ward	678	188
Chicago, Milwaukee, St. Paul	678	787
Phillips Petroleum	667	145
Philadelphia Electric	667	384
American Tobacco	657	265
Illinois Central	657	729
Kennecott Copper	631	338
Norfolk & Western	585	542
Southern Company	580	–
Aluminum Company	575	235
Detroit Edison	575	296
R. J. Reynolds Tobacco	554	163
Republic Steel	552	332
Louisville & Nashville	543	545
Southern Calif. Edison	538	340
United Fruit	516	226
Chicago & Northwestern	513	690

Spectacular gains in assets over 1929 are shown by several corporations, including Creole Petroleum and Commercial Credit. The assets of Chrysler tripled, and those of General Electric and duPont doubled.

There is no way of knowing whether the same ratio of corporate asset growth will be registered in the next twenty years. Assuming such ratio growth does continue, the young man or woman buying, in periods of low prices, sound common stocks in basic industries, stocks with long dividend records, would be reasonably sure of maximum yield and very substantial capital enhancement.

It is the reckless get-rich-quick boys who go broke in the stock market.

Hungry eyes from other lands look upon the miracle of America with growing wonderment.

Iron curtains and bamboo curtains cannot wholly conceal the story of the rise of the little man, the little capitalist, the man with insurance, a home, a car, and some shares of corporation stock.

To a surprising degree we are becoming a nation of small capitalists. In recent years this group has jacked up its stake in basic industries. A list of stockholders of most any large corporation is a study in democratic growth, for it etches in sharp outline the picture of the little man, thrifty and prudent, taking his place with the wealthy in ownership of far-flung properties.

Curiously, this forward impulse, under free government, was especially marked right in a period when charlatans and mountebanks, liars and swindlers, were spreading their poisonous doctrines of communism, socialism and fascism across broad stretches of the earth.

It expanded in the very period when the great British Empire was cracking up, stumbling in darkness, when the dead hand of England's socialist adventurers was weighing down on a people steeped in the traditions of freedom. Today England's tragic experiment stands as a monumental warning to the English and to other liberty-loving peoples.

America, too, has had its political clowns and fakers, its quacks, humbugs and rabble-rousers; they come out of the shadows in times of stress and stir class wars and hatred and prejudices; they defame principles of justice and spatter mud on the machinery of democracy. Always their false promises may be distilled to the single thought: "Trust us. Give us complete power (and your money) and we'll make every man a king."

You may rake the records of history without finding a single instance where the common man's reward was other than distress from the grant of vast power and the payment of towering taxes.

There is nothing basically wrong with America, nothing aside from the growing, frightening tendency to impose intolerable taxes in times of peace.

Our magnificent financial system — our banks, insurance companies, our excellent stock and commodity exchanges — stand a mighty rock in a sea of world disorder.

Mistakes of the past have been admitted, corrective measures have been taken, and "Wall Street," as a symbol of freedom of trade by free men, will endure in the changing patterns of America's bold onward drive to a broader and greater destiny.